Hiking Ozarks

A Guide to the Area's
Greatest Hiking Adventures

JD Tanner and Emily Ressler-Tanner

FALCONGUIDES

GUILFORD, CONNECTICUT
HELENA, MONTANA
AN IMPRINT OF GLOBE PEQUOT PRESS

FALCONGUIDES®

Copyright © 2014 Morris Book Publishing, LLC

ALL RIGHTS RESERVED. No part of this book may be reproduced or transmitted in any form by any means, electronic or mechanical, including photocopying and recording, or by any information storage and retrieval system, except as may be expressly permitted in writing from the publisher. Requests for permission should be addressed to Globe Pequot Press, Attn: Rights and Permissions Department, PO Box 480, Guilford, CT 06437.

FalconGuides is an imprint of Globe Pequot Press.
Falcon, FalconGuides, and Outfit Your Mind are registered trademarks of Morris Book Publishing, LLC.

All interior photos by JD Tanner and Emily Ressler-Tanner

Maps by Mapping Specialists © Morris Book Publishing, LLC
Layout: Sue Murray
Project editor: Meredith Dias

Library of Congress Cataloging-in-Publication Data is available on file.

ISBN 978-0-7627-8239-0

Printed in the United States of America

10 9 8 7 6 5 4 3 2 1

Contents

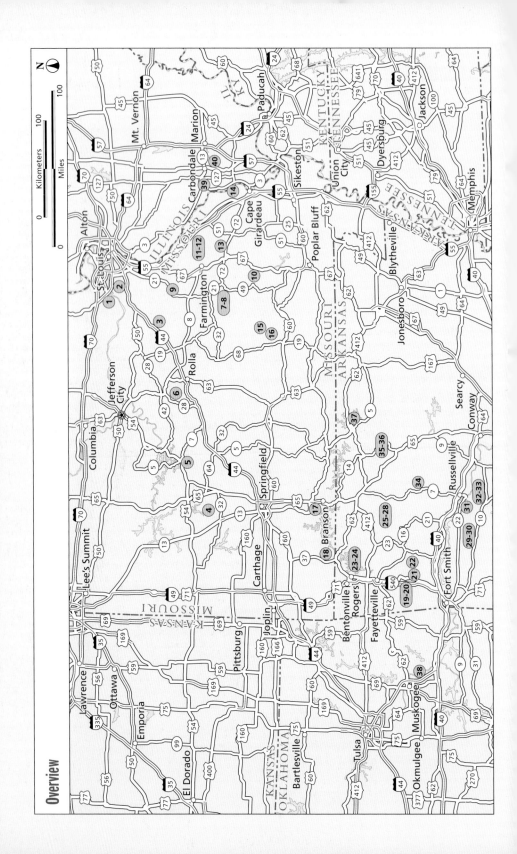

Overview

ACKNOWLEDGMENTS

We would like to send out a special thank you to all the land managers who patiently answered our questions, pointed us toward the very best trails, and carefully reviewed the trail descriptions for this guide. We would also like to thank our friends and family for accompanying us on many of the trails in the Ozarks; your company, humor, support, and enthusiasm were very much appreciated. Finally we would like to thank all of our friends at Falcon Guides, particularly Katie Benoit, Max Phelps, and Meredith Dias, for their support and encouragement and for making a book out of our rough manuscript.

JD Tanner and Emily Ressler-Tanner

INTRODUCTION

The Ozarks are a physiographic and geologic highland region of the central United States. They cover much of the southern half of Missouri and an extensive portion of northwestern and north-central Arkansas. This is a vast region, covering over 60,000 square acres and spreading across Arkansas, Missouri, Oklahoma, and Kansas. Some argue that the region also includes southern Illinois. While the boundaries of the Ozarks are somewhat muddled, the name of the region itself is even more confusing. Depending on who is describing the area, you may here the region referred to as the Ozark Mountains, the Ozark Highlands, the Ozark Upland, the Ozark Hills, the Ozark Hill Country, the Ozark Plateau, or the Ozarks (as we refer to the region in this guide). Given the large geographical area, the diversity of scenery, the sporadic pockets of populated areas, and the unique vernacular of those who live here, it is easy to see how labeling the area with just one title has been a challenge.

Once a large plateau, the Ozarks are not particularly high in elevation. The most mountain-like areas include the St. Francois Mountains in Missouri and the Boston Mountains in Arkansas. The region is characterized by a wealth of springs, caves, and sinkholes and owes its unique characteristics to the power of erosion. Over time water has changed the plateau, carving away portions of the soil and the underlying sedimentary rocks and leaving the hills, valleys, exposed bluffs, and fascinating rock formations that we see today.

We couldn't be more excited to introduce you to the extensive network of trails offered here in the Ozarks. This is a landscape that offers endless beauty and solitude for outdoor enthusiasts. Hikes across long ridgetops, into quiet valleys and cool hollows, and through rocky creeks give visitors a chance to view the unique natural and cultural history of the area. Springs, caves, sinkholes, bluffs, glades, hardwood forests, clear-flowing streams, waterfalls, and lakes are the natural gems of the Ozarks and are all highlighted in this guide.

If you are a visitor to the Ozarks, this collection of hiking trails will serve as a valued tool in becoming familiar with the great variety of outdoor adventures within this vast region. Our hope is that this guide will serve as your introduction to Ozark adventures and will keep you returning to the Ozark backwoods time and time again. If you are a longtime local of the area, this book will hopefully take you on some new adventures to some lesser-known trails in this diverse region.

This guide lists easy, moderate, and more challenging hikes in the Ozarks. Some of the hikes can be found near more-populated areas such as St. Louis, Cape Girardeau, Springfield, and Fayetteville. Visitors to the region will find trails near the most popular vacation destinations such as the Buffalo National River, Branson, and Lake of the Ozarks. Most are nestled in the heart of the Missouri and Arkansas Ozarks and will likely require a bit of driving to find the trailhead. All showcase the natural wonders hidden in this region. From the highest elevations in Arkansas and Missouri to the tallest waterfall between the Appalachian and Rocky Mountains, the hikes featured in the pages of this book are some of best hikes in the region. We have done our best to include a little something for everyone and have tried to select trails from every part of the region while still making sure to include those trails widely considered to be superior for their scenic and historical significance. Hikes for families, for nature lovers, for scenic views, and for history buffs have all been included and should be considered an introduction to the areas and a starting point to continue your explorations in the Ozarks.

Weather

The weather in the Ozarks consists of a mild spring, ranging from cool to warm and muggy, that is typically wet. Trail conditions can be quite muddy during spring, especially for hikes that are in or near floodplains. The biggest concern for spring weather in the Ozarks is the chance for thunder/lightning storms, hail, and/or tornadoes.

Storms still pose a threat in early summer, but as the summer progresses the weather tends to be less wet and sometimes very hot and almost always humid. Hikers that choose to get out in the mid- to late summer might consider early-morning hikes, as high temperatures and humidity usually set in by midmorning.

Fall can be downright gorgeous in the Ozarks. The mostly hardwood forests often exhibit a dazzling array of fall colors. Daytime temperatures in the low to mid-70s

Lightning storm in southern Missouri

along with decreased humidity make for some amazingly scenic hikes. Fall hiking cannot be encouraged enough.

The Ozarks have an abundance of cold and snowy days in winter, but if you don't mind hiking with no leaves on the trees, winter can be a very enjoyable time to hike here as well. Wintertime hikers will get more views of the rolling hills. The unusual rock formations are made even more magical after a light dusting of snow, and hikers will typically enjoy the trails almost all to themselves.

Ideal times for hiking in the Ozarks are early to late spring and mid- to late fall. Mix in the handful of cool days in summer and warm winter days and a person can enjoy many picture-perfect hiking days in the Ozarks each year.

Weather Averages for Springfield, Missouri

Month	High (°F)	Low (°F)	Rainfall (Inches)
January	43	22	2.47
February	48	26	2.62
March	58	35	3.62
April	67	44	4.32
May	75	54	5.10
June	84	63	4.85
July	89	68	3.68
August	89	67	3.55
September	80	58	4.61
October	69	47	3.59
November	57	35	4.22
December	45	25	3.04

(Statistics from the Weather Channel, June 2013)

Flora and Fauna

The Ozarks are home to an incredible number of both plant and animal species. The Ozarks provide several types of unique habitats to foster this ecological diversity. Woodlands, open fields, swamp-like areas, rivers and streams, caves, bluffs, glades, and even abandoned buildings provide important habitat for the species that live here. Many of the mammals here are nocturnal and skilled at avoiding humans. The best times to catch a glimpse of these critters are the early morning and at dusk. Hikers here are likely to see opossums, skunks, squirrels, rabbits, armadillos, white-tailed deer, raccoons, and possibly black bear, gray fox, elk, and bobcats. There have been a handful of confirmed mountain lion sightings in the region, but the chance of seeing one is incredibly unlikely.

The Ozarks are also an outstanding attraction for birding fanatics—over 400 species of birds can be spotted here! Great blue herons, belted kingfishers, and wood

Ozark wild crocus

ducks are common sights along many of the rivers in the region. Bald eagles are frequently observed in the trees along ridgetops during the winter months. Visitors might be surprised to spot a roadrunner in dry glades or along the Buffalo River. Northern cardinals, chickadees, hummingbirds, titmice, wrens, and woodpeckers are common in almost every part of the Ozarks.

Do watch your step when hiking the trails of the Ozarks. There are many species of nonvenomous snakes found here and several species of venomous snakes, including copperheads, cottonmouths, pygmy rattlesnakes, and timber rattlesnakes. All snakes serve an important ecological purpose in controlling the population of rodents and other pests. The copperhead and timber rattlesnake are the venomous snakes a hiker is most likely to encounter along trails. Venomous snakes are most easily recognized by their "arrow-shaped" heads. To avoid being bitten, hikers should wear protective footwear, never place hands under rocks or logs, keep an eye on the ground as they hike, and never attempt to handle or kill snakes. Snakebites are incredibly rare and are usually the result of a person attempting to handle a snake. Pay attention to where you are walking, particularly along rocky slopes and near waterways, and you shouldn't have any problems. Leave them alone and they will leave you alone.

There is also a wide diversity of plant life found in the Ozarks. Woodland forests are dominated by oak and hickory, but you'll also find shortleaf pine, sycamore, cottonwood, birch, maple, redbud, dogwood, and cedar. Spring brings the enjoyment of wildflower blooms, which last for several months. Look for more common species such as larkspur, purple coneflower, and columbine. Showy lady's slipper and rein orchid are two beautiful and rare wildflowers that can be found in the Ozarks. The Ozark wild crocus is a particularly beautiful flower that is only found in the Ozarks. It blooms in April and May in densely wooded areas along the Current River.

Allium stellatum, *or wild onion, can be found in dry, rocky glades throughout the Ozarks.*

Wilderness Restrictions/Regulations

The hiking trails in this book traverse through lands that are controlled and managed by various public agencies. Each group has their own rules and regulations that must be respected and adhered to at all times while hiking on these lands. The trails in this book cross through lands managed by the United States Forest Service, the National Park Service, Missouri State Parks, Arkansas State Parks, Oklahoma State Parks, Missouri Department of Conservation, and St. Louis County Parks. Hikes on lands managed by the National Park Service will have firmer rules and regulations with regard to recreation and land-use restrictions.

When day hiking you generally do not need permits to enjoy any of the trails in this book, although many land managers do request that you register at the trailhead. If you plan to embark on a long-distance hiking trip, you should call the managing office of the area through which you are hiking and secure a backcountry permit for the area. You may be required to reserve your campsites for each night that you will be camping along the trail. USFS lands are typically less strict about camping and usually allow dispersed, primitive camping along the trails as long as you are not within a particular distance from waterways, the trail, roads, and other specified areas. Before

Before hiking, be sure to register at the trailhead.

embarking on a hiking trip, plan ahead by checking the website or calling the office of the management agency of the lands you will be traversing. They will provide the most up-to-date information on regulations and trail conditions.

Hazards

There are a few hazards to be aware of and to prepare for when hiking in the Ozarks. **Poison ivy,** a year-round hazard, might be the most common and most annoying issue hikers will come across while hiking here. Poison ivy has been found throughout the Ozarks, and it is estimated that somewhere between 50 and 70 percent of people experience a physical reaction after coming in contact with the plant. Poison ivy can grow as a woody shrub up to 6 feet high or as a vine that clings to other trees and shrubs. While the old expression "Leaves of three, let it be" is good advice to follow, several other three-leaf plants grow in the Ozarks, so be sure to educate yourself about poison ivy before hitting the trail. If you are particularly sensitive to the plant, it is a good idea to keep a bottle of poison ivy soap in your vehicle and wash all exposed skin upon completion of your hike. Be sure to launder all hiking clothes separate from other clothes and in hot water to remove the poison ivy oils. Poison ivy can be found on almost every hike in this book.

Ticks are most abundant in the region during spring and summer. There are many different types of ticks, but the two most common in the Ozarks are the Lone Star tick and the American dog tick. Ticks have been known to carry, and occasionally spread, the organisms that cause Lyme disease, Rocky Mountain spotted fever, and tularemia. Ticks are unavoidable but are no reason to avoid hiking in spring and summer. Hikers should wear lighter-colored clothing to help detect ticks, use repellent that is proven effective against ticks, periodically check for ticks during your hike, and perform a complete body check on yourself and your pet after every hike. During spring and summer ticks can be found on every hike in this book.

Poison ivy

There are at least fifty different species of **mosquitoes** in the Ozarks, and the most common concern with mosquitoes is the West Nile virus. It is estimated that only 1 percent of mosquitoes carry West Nile virus, and only 1 percent of people bitten will actually contract the virus. Like ticks, mosquitoes should not be a reason to avoid hiking in spring or summer. Simply be aware and be prepared. To help you avoid mosquitoes, use insect repellent, wear long pants and long-sleeved shirts, avoid hiking at dawn or dusk, and don't wear perfume or cologne when hiking. Mosquitoes can be found on every hike in this book.

Venomous snakes are the fourth hazard hikers might encounter on the hikes in this book. Most of the snakes in the Ozarks are harmless; however, hikers should be aware that several species of venomous snakes do inhabit the area. Your chances of being bitten by a venomous snake in the United States are very, very low. Fewer than 8,000 people are bitten every year by a venomous snake, most while trying to handle or kill the snake, and fewer than five of those people die.

Other hazards you may encounter include (but are not limited to) steep drop-offs along bluffs, thunder/lightning storms, tornadoes, a growing population of black bears, and heat-related illnesses. As mentioned earlier, many of the hikes in this guide are in rural areas. Having a full tank of gas and being aware of the nearest medical facility are highly recommended.

Be Prepared

"Be prepared." The Boy Scouts say it, Leave No Trace says it, and the best outdoors people say it. Being prepared won't completely keep you out of harm's way when outdoors, but it will minimize the chances of finding yourself there. That being said, here are some things to consider:

- Speak with local land managers to get the most up-to-date information on road and trail conditions.
- Familiarize yourself with the basics of first aid (bites, stings, sprains, and breaks), and carry a first-aid kit and know how to use it.
- Hydrate! No matter where or when you are hiking, you should always be carrying water with you. A standard is two liters per person per day.
- Be prepared to treat water on longer hikes. Rivers and streams are not safe to drink directly from in the Ozarks area. Iodine tablets are small, light, and easy to carry.
- Carry a backpack in order to store the Ten Essentials: map, compass, sunglasses/sunscreen, extra food and water, extra clothes, headlamp/flashlight, first-aid kit, fire starter, matches, and knife.
- Pack your cell phone (on vibrate) as a safety backup.
- Keep an eye on the kids. Having them carry a whistle, just in case, isn't the worst idea.
- Bring a leash, doggie bags, and extra water for your pets.

Leave No Trace

This hiking guide will take you to historical sites, conservation areas, national natural landmarks, and many other places of natural and cultural significance. For that reason, the importance of Leave No Trace cannot be stressed enough. You are encouraged to carefully plan your trip so that you know as much as you possibly can about the area you will be visiting. Being aware of information such as the weather forecast, trail conditions, and water availability is an important factor to planning a successful trip.

Once you begin your hike, do your best to stick to trails so you do not inadvertently trample sensitive vegetation. Be prepared to pack out any trash that you bring with you and remember: It never hurts to carry out trash that others may have left behind. Be extra careful when visiting sites of historical and natural importance. Leave everything as you found it, and never remove artifacts found in these sensitive areas.

Consider your impact on wildlife as you visit their homes, and be sure not to feed them, as this act is unhealthy for wildlife and dangerous for people. Respect other visitors and users as well by keeping your pet on a leash, stepping to the side of the trail to allow others to pass, and by keeping noise to a minimum.

For more information on enjoying the outdoors responsibly, please visit the Leave No Trace Center for Outdoor Ethics website at LNT.org.

Each region begins with a section intro, where you're given a sweeping look at the lay of the land. After this general overview, specific hikes within that region are described. You'll learn about the terrain and what surprises each route has to offer.

This guide is designed to be simple and easy to use. Each hike is described with a map and summary information that delivers the trail's vital statistics including length, difficulty, fees and permits, park hours, canine compatibility, and trail contacts. Directions to the trailhead are also provided, along with a general description of what you'll see along the way. A detailed route finder (Miles and Directions) sets forth mileages between significant landmarks along the trail.

How the Hikes Were Chosen

This guide describes trails that are accessible to every hiker, whether visiting from out of town or a local resident. The hikes in this guide range in length from just over 1 mile to over 26 miles, and most are in the 4- to 8-mile range. Hikes range in difficulty from flat excursions perfect for a family outing to more challenging treks in the rolling hills of the Ozarks. While these trails are among the best, keep in mind that nearby trails, sometimes in the same park or sometimes in a neighboring open space, may offer options better suited to your needs. We've tried to include other great hikes in the Honorable Mentions sections of the guide.

Selecting a Hike

Some would argue that no hike involving any kind of climbing is easy, but climbs are a fact of life in the Ozarks region. Trail difficulty is a highly subjective matter, but we've tried to give you an idea of what to expect on each hike. Below is a description of how trail difficulty is categorized for this guide.

Easy hikes are generally short and flat, taking no longer than an hour to complete.

Moderate hikes involve increased distance and relatively mild changes in elevation, and will take one to two hours to complete.

More challenging hikes feature some steep stretches, greater distances, and generally take longer than two hours to complete.

Keep in mind that what you think is easy is entirely dependent on your level of fitness and the adequacy of your gear (primarily shoes). Use the trail's length as a gauge of its relative difficulty—even if climbing is involved, it won't be too strenuous if the hike is less than 1 mile long. If you are hiking with a group, select a hike that's appropriate for the least fit and prepared in your party.

Hiking times are based on the assumption that on flat ground, most walkers average 2 miles per hour. Adjust that rate by the steepness of the terrain and your level of fitness (subtract time if you're an aerobic animal and add time if you're hiking with kids), and you have a ballpark hiking duration. Be sure to add more time if you plan to picnic or take part in other activities like bird watching, swimming, wandering, or photography.

Trail Finder

Best Backpacking
3. Meramec State Park: Wilderness Trail
8. Ozark Trail: Taum Sauk Mountain State Park to Johnson's Shut-Ins State Park
23. Hobbs State Park: Pigeon Roost Trail
35. Buffalo National River: Buffalo River Trail—Spring Creek Section
38. Greenleaf State Park: Greenleaf Lake Hiking Trail

Best Hikes for Waterfalls
7. Taum Sauk Mountain State Park: Mina Sauk Falls Loop Trail/Ozark Trail to Devil's Tollgate
16. Ozark Trail: Klepzig Mill to Rocky Falls
25. Buffalo National River: Lost Valley Trail
26. Buffalo National River: Centerpoint Trailhead to Hemmed-In Hollow
27. Buffalo National River: Compton Trailhead to Hemmed-In Hollow
32. Petit Jean State Park: Cedar Falls Trail

Best Hikes for Geology Lovers
5. Ha Ha Tonka State Park: Devil's Kitchen Trail
6. Clifty Creek Natural Area and Clifty Creek Conservation Area: Clifty Creek Trail
7. Taum Sauk Mountain State Park: Mina Sauk Falls Loop Trail/Ozark Trail to Devil's Tollgate
11. Pickle Springs Natural Area: Trail Through Time
20. Devil's Den State Park: Devil's Den Trail
33. Petit Jean State Park: Seven Hollows Trail
34. Ozark National Forest: Pedestal Rocks Trail
36. Buffalo National River: Indian Rockhouse Trail
39. Shawnee National Forest: Little Grand Canyon Trail
40. Shawnee National Forest: Panther Den Trail

Best Hikes for Children
11. Pickle Springs Natural Area: Trail Through Time
13. Amidon Memorial Conservation Area: Cedar Glade Trail
15. Blue Spring Natural Area: Blue Springs Trail
18. Roaring River State Park: Fire Tower Trail
20. Devil's Den State Park: Devil's Den Trail
36. Buffalo National River: Indian Rockhouse Trail
37. Norfork Lake Recreation Area: Robinson Point Trail
40. Shawnee National Forest: Panther Den Trail

Best Hikes for Great Views

14. Trail of Tears State Park: Sheppard Point Trail
19. Devil's Den State Park: Yellow Rock Trail
22. White Rock Mountain Recreation Area: Rim Trail
26. Buffalo National River: Centerpoint Trailhead to Hemmed-In Hollow
28. Ozark National Forest: Whitaker Point Trail
30. Mount Magazine State Park: Highpoint Loop Trails
35. Buffalo National River: Buffalo River Trail—Spring Creek Section

Best Hikes for History Lovers

1. Weldon Spring Conservation Area: Lewis Trail
9. Washington State Park: Rockywood Trail
17. Ruth and Paul Henning Conservation Area: Homesteaders Trail
31. Mount Nebo State Park: Bench Road Trail
36. Buffalo National River: Indian Rockhouse Trail

Best Hikes for Nature Lovers

2. Lone Elk County Park: White Bison Trail
4. Pomme de Terre State Park: Indian Point Trail
9. Washington State Park: Rockywood Trail
10. Sam A. Baker State Park: Mudlick Mountain Trail
11. Pickle Springs Natural Area: Trail Through Time
12. Hawn State Park: Whispering Pines Trail—North Loop
18. Roaring River State Park: Fire Tower Trail
21. Ozark Highlands Trail: Lake Fort Smith State Park to Frogg Bayou
24. Hobbs State Park: Bashore Ridge Loop Trail
29. Mount Magazine State Park: Bear Hollow Trail

Map Legend

Municipal

≡(44)≡ Interstate Highway

≡(65)≡ US Highway

≡(94)≡ State Road

═══════ Local/County Road

= = = = Unpaved Road

─ ─ · ─ · County Boundary

─ ─ · · ─ · State Boundary

Trails

▪▪▪▪▪▪ Featured Trail

─ ─ ─ ─ Trail

Water Features

Body of Water

River/Creek

Intermittent Stream

Waterfall

Spring

Land Management

National Park/Forest

National Monument/Wilderness Area

State/County Park

Symbols

≍ Bridge

▪ Building/Point of Interest

▲ Campground

∩ Cave

🅿 Parking

▲ Peak/Elevation

🌐 Picnic Area

📷 Ranger Station/Park Office

🚻 Restroom

📷 Scenic View

🗼 Tower

○ Town

① Trailhead

❓ Visitor/Information Center

Missouri Region

The Missouri Ozarks form all of the northern and much of the eastern and western boundaries of the Ozarks. Easy access from several midsize and large cities, including Kansas City, Columbia, St. Louis, Cape Girardeau, and Springfield, make hiking in the Missouri region of the Ozarks fairly accessible. Most of the hikes in the Missouri region are within a few short hours of these populated areas. Several of the hikes are located closer to tourist destinations such as Lake of the Ozarks and Branson. While the hikes are close in proximity to these city centers, most of the hikes seem incredibly remote.

The highlights of the Missouri region include dense woodlands; numerous crystal-clear rivers, creeks, and springs; dry, desertlike glades; and fantastic rock formations that have been carved out of this rugged and challenging landscape over many, many years. Eighteen of the trails in this book are found scattered throughout the Missouri Ozarks. In 2013 Missouri was named the "Best Trails State" by American Trails, a national nonprofit organization working on behalf of the nation's hiking, biking, and riding trails. The national award is presented every two years to a state that has made tremendous contributions to promote and improve their trail system. This is most certainly a deserved title to the state of Missouri, and you will find many new trails being developed and many old trails being maintained and improved.

Many of the trails found in the Missouri region are in state parks. Missouri State Parks offers nearly 1,000 miles of managed trails. The state also contains more than 500 miles of designated National Recreation Trails, the 360-mile Ozark Trail, and the 225-mile Katy Trail. Hiking here seems to only be getting better!

1 Weldon Spring Conservation Area: Lewis Trail

This loop hike takes you through the Weldon Spring Conservation Area at the northern tip of the Ozark Plateau. Towering limestone bluffs offering excellent views of the Missouri River, an abundance of wildlife, and easy access from Saint Louis combine to make for an ideal day trip.

Start: From the Weldon Spring Conservation Area parking lot and Lewis & Clark Trailhead
Distance: 8.2-mile loop
Hiking time: About 4 hours
Difficulty: More challenging due to length and demanding climbs
Trail surface: Forested trail
Best season: Fall through spring
Other trail users: Hikers only

Canine compatibility: Leashed dogs permitted
Fees and permits: None
Schedule: Open year-round
Maps: USGS Weldon Spring; park map and brochure available at the visitor center
Trail contacts: Missouri Department of Conservation, St. Louis Regional Office, 2360 Highway D, St. Charles, MO 63304; (636) 441-4554; http://mdc.mo.gov

Finding the trailhead: From St. Louis, drive almost 29 miles on I-64 West/US 40 West to MO 94 West at exit 10. Turn left onto MO 94 and drive 2.4 miles to the Weldon Spring Conservation Area parking lot and Lewis and Clark Trailhead. GPS: N38 42.445' / W90 43.452'

The Hike

Located in Saint Charles County, the 8,359-acre Weldon Spring Conservation Area offers a variety of natural features, including large plots of forests, tall limestone bluffs, wetlands, glades, pastures, and some agricultural lands. This combination of habitats makes for a diverse collection of flora and fauna in the area, despite a close proximity to the city. White-tailed deer, wild turkeys, raccoons, squirrels, foxes, and five-lined skink (a type of lizard) are just some of the wild animals that flourish here. The southern border of the area is formed by the Missouri River. The Katy Trail, a 225-mile biking and walking trail, cuts across the southern portion of Weldon Spring Conservation Area.

Located next to the information kiosk, the Clark Trail begins on the eastern end of the parking area. The trailhead is marked with a wooden CLARK TRAIL 5.3 MILES sign and a LEWIS TRAIL 8.2 MILES sign. Begin hiking north on the obvious path, passing eastern red cedar, roughleaf dogwood, honey locust, and eastern redbud trees. After 0.1 mile the trail forks. Stay right (south), following the white arrow.

At 1.3 miles you gain sight of the Missouri River and come to an interpretive sign, which gives historical information on the Lewis and Clark expedition. Follow the trail as it turns sharply to the left (north).

View of Missouri River from Lewis Trail

After climbing a moderately steep ridge, pass several scenic overlooks at 2.2 miles. The impressive limestone bluffs tower above the Missouri River and the famous Katy Trail. From here the trail descends the ridge to a dry creek bottom at 2.8 miles. Cross the creek and follow its bank to the intersection of the Clark Trail and the Lewis Trail. Stay right (east) to continue on the Lewis Trail.

The trail follows an old fence line (3.3 miles) along the bluffs before descending again via a series of mellow switchbacks through a mostly maple-and-oak forest. The trail crosses a small footbridge at 5.4 miles and then an access road at 5.6 miles.

At 6.4 miles the trail rejoins the Clark Trail. Stay right (north) at this intersection to complete the loop. Cross another footbridge at 7.0 miles and continue southwest. Arrive back at the trailhead at 8.2 miles.

Lewis Trail

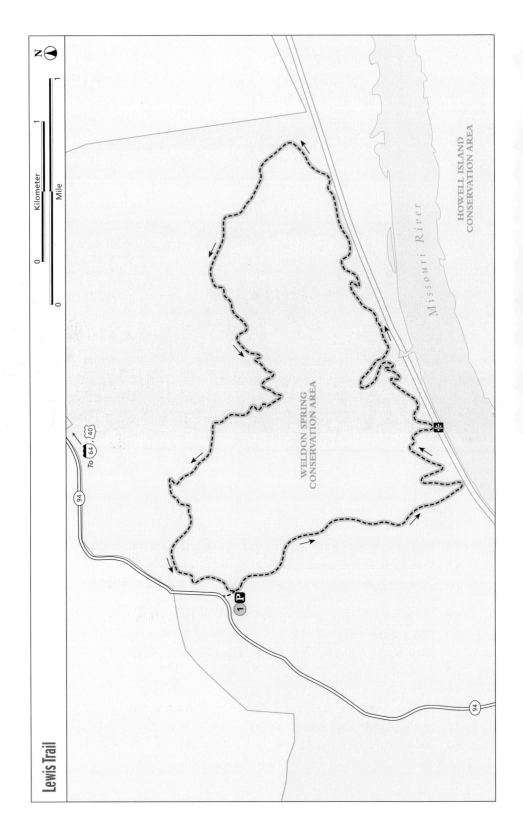

N

0   Kilometer   1

0   Mile   1

94

To 64 , 40

WELDON SPRING
CONSERVATION AREA

1 P

Missouri River

HOWELL ISLAND
CONSERVATION AREA

94

Lewis Trail

Miles and Directions

0.0 From the trailhead, begin hiking southeast on the Lewis Trail and the Clark Trail.

0.1 At the fork in the trail, turn right (south) to stay on the Lewis and Clark Trails.

1.3 Come to the Lewis and Clark interpretive sign and follow the trail as it curves to the left (north).

2.2 After ascending a moderately steep ridge, come to a series of overlooks.

2.8 Cross a dry creek bottom.

3.3 Follow the trail as it parallels an old fence line along limestone bluffs.

5.4 Cross a small footbridge.

5.6 Cross an access road.

6.4 At the intersection with the Clark Trail, stay right (north) to complete the loop.

7.0 Cross a footbridge and continue southwest.

8.2 Return to the trailhead parking area.

2 Lone Elk County Park: White Bison Trail

Herds of elk and buffalo are undoubtedly an uncommon occurrence in St. Louis County, yet a trip to Lone Elk County Park can offer wildlife lovers sightings of both. The White Bison Trail presents wildlife viewing opportunities rarely seen in this part of the country. The 3.0-mile loop trail travels through the gated county park that is home to several elk and buffalo. Elk are commonly seen along the hiking trail.

Start: From the Lone Elk County Park Visitor Center parking area
Distance: 3.0-mile loop
Hiking time: About 2 hours
Difficulty: Moderate due to modest climbs
Trail surface: Forested trail
Best season: Fall through spring
Other trail users: Hikers only

Canine compatibility: No dogs permitted in park or on trails
Fees and permits: None
Schedule: Open year-round
Maps: USGS Manchester; trail map available at visitor center
Trail contacts: Lone Elk County Park, 1 Lone Elk Park Rd., Valley Park, MO 63088; (314) 615-4386; www.stlouisco.com/parks

Finding the trailhead: From St. Louis, take I-44 West for 17 miles to MO 141 (exit 272). Merge onto North Highway Drive, take a slight right onto MO 141, and then take the ramp to the North Outer Road. Turn left onto Meramec Street and stay straight onto West Outer Road for 2 miles. Turn right onto Lone Elk Park Road. Drive 0.6 mile to the park entrance on the left and drive 0.2 mile more before staying left at the fork. Follow the road for another 0.3 mile, where you will reach the visitor center, parking area, and trailhead. Modern restrooms and water are available at the visitor center. GPS: N38 31.873' / W90 32.600'

The Hike

Lone Elk County Park is an interesting park with a peculiar past that makes for a memorable day trip for hikers in and around St. Louis. Part of a large cattle operation in the 1800s, the area that now makes up Lone Elk Park was purchased by the Military Department in 1941 and used as an ammunition depot until the end of World War II. After the war the area was declared a surplus and the park was taken over by St. Louis County Parks. Taking advantage of the 8-foot-tall perimeter fence, the new park was stocked with ten elk from Yellowstone National Park. In 1951 the park was taken over by the Department of the Army and used once again for military purposes. By the end of the 1950s, the elk herd had grown to more than one hundred and was beginning to run out of food. With winter approaching, it was decided that all the elk would be exterminated and the meat donated to local hospitals. One lone bull

Bull elk on White Bison Trail

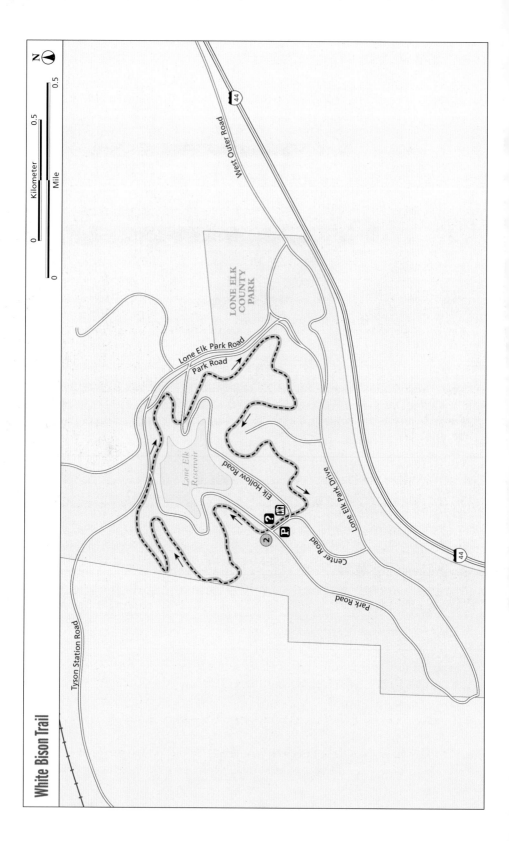

White Bison Trail

White Bison Trail

escaped this fate and roamed the hills alone for several years. In 1963 the area was taken over by Washington University, and in 1966 students from Rockwood School District partnered with the West St. Louis Lions club to purchase more elk from Yellowstone National Park, bringing the lone elk some much needed company after eight years of solitude.

Today, hikers coming to Lone Elk County Park can expect to see elk, white-tailed deer, wild turkeys, waterfowl, and bison. The forest is a typical Missouri hardwood mix, full of oaks and hickories. If visitors want to extend their trip, they can pay a visit to the World Bird Sanctuary to see bald eagles, hawks, owls, and more.

The White Bison Trail loops around Lone Elk Reservoir and hikers will more than likely pass right by the elk herds that rest near the trail. Visitors will have to enjoy the bison from their vehicles, as the herd is kept separate from the rest of the park.

From the visitor center parking area, locate the White Bison Trail on the west side of Lone Elk Park Road. The trail begins just across a small footbridge, near the picnic area, and is marked with a white buffalo trail marker. The trail ascends a steep, rocky slope and curves northeast through hickory, oak, maples, and redbuds. The trail passes through a woodland area, which includes an abundance of pawpaw trees. The trail bends sharply to the right (north) at 0.9 mile and descends the hill.

At 1.1 miles you'll come to a park road and turn right (east). Follow the road for 0.1 mile, crossing Lone Elk Park Road and following the trail east into the woods (the lake is to the south of the trail). Cross Elk Hollow Road and a picnic area at 1.6 miles and continue following the trail south. At 2.0 miles the trail turns to the right (west). Come to another park road at 2.9 miles. The visitor center and trailhead parking area is just ahead (west). Arrive at the visitor center and trailhead parking area at 3.0 miles.

Miles and Directions

0.0 From the footbridge, begin hiking west.

0.9 The trail bends sharply to the right (north) and descends the hill.

1.1 Come to a park road and turn right (east), following the road up a short hill.

1.2 Cross Lone Elk Park Road and continue east into the woods.

1.6 Cross Elk Hollow Road and a picnic area.

2.0 Follow the trail as it curves to the west.

2.9 Cross park road and continue west toward the visitor center.

3.0 Return to the visitor center and parking area.

3 Meramec State Park: Wilderness Trail

The Wilderness Trail in Meramec State Park is a beautiful 8.6-mile hike through a portion of the park's 6,896 acres. While the park offers several miles of hiking/backpacking trails and numerous backcountry campsites, the caves tend to be the biggest draw to the park. More than forty caves grace the area, including the popular Fisher Cave.

Start: Wilderness Trail parking area in Meramec State Park

Distance: 8.6-mile loop

Hiking time: About 5 hours

Difficulty: More challenging due to length

Trail surface: Forested trail

Best season: Spring through fall

Other trail users: Hikers only

Canine compatibility: Leashed dogs permitted

Fees and permits: None

Schedule: Open year-round

Maps: USGS Meramec State Park; trail map available at the park office

Trail contacts: Meramec State Park, 115 Meramec Park Dr., Sullivan, MO 63080; (573) 468-6072, www.mostateparks.com/park/meramec-state-park

Finding the trailhead: From Sullivan, Missouri, take MO 185 south and drive 3.3 miles to the park entrance on the right. Follow Meramec Drive for 0.3 mile and turn left at the stop sign. After 1 mile turn left into the parking area for the Wilderness Trail. GPS: N38 12.766' / W91 05.609'

The Hike

Located on the northern perimeter of the Ozarks, the 6,896-acre Meramec State Park is one of Missouri's natural treasures. Flanked on the east side by the Meramec River, this area is known for rich glades, mature hardwood forests, and numerous caves. Wildlife is abundant in the park and you may encounter bobcats, white-tailed deer, and even black bears as you explore this area. Some of the caves are open to exploration and you may encounter rare species of bats in some of these caves.

The Wilderness Trail is the longest trail in the park and the only trail designated for backpacking. Eight backpacking camps are provided along the trail, although for hikers looking for a more challenging day hike, it is possible to hike the trail in a single day. If you choose to hike on the Wilderness Trail, you will not be disappointed as the trail cuts through the most rugged and remote areas of the park. From the Meramec Upland Forest Natural Area to Copper Hollow and Copper Hollow Spring, this area is diverse, and new sights seem to appear around every bend in the trail.

From the Wilderness Trail parking area and trailhead, begin hiking north on the Wilderness Trail. At 0.2 mile you will reach the trail register, where you should sign in and continue hiking west. You will reach the loop portion of the

Wilderness Trail

trail at 0.4 mile. Bear left (northwest) and make your way past the first of two backcountry campsites at 0.6 and 0.7 miles. Pass the trail access to the campsites and make your way into and out of Campbell Hollow before reaching and crossing MO Spur Route 185 at 2.0 miles.

Continue hiking north and pass by a white-blazed connector trail on the right at 2.4 miles before you reach a series of backcountry campsites at miles 2.5, 3.3, 3.4, and 3.7. After the last backcountry campsite, the trail begins a steep descent down into Copper Hollow. As the hollow opens up at 4.3 miles, you'll come to Copper Hollow Spring. From the spring, continue hiking east to catch a quick glimpse of the Meramec River before the trail turns west.

At 6.2 miles you will reach the white-blazed connector trail again and then cross MO Spur Route 185 again at 6.8 miles. Hike southeast after crossing the road toward the last backcountry campsite at 7.4 miles, then cross Ridge Road (a service road) at 7.7 miles. The trail continues south and then southeast to the end of the loop at 8.2 miles. Return to the trailhead and parking area at 8.6 miles.

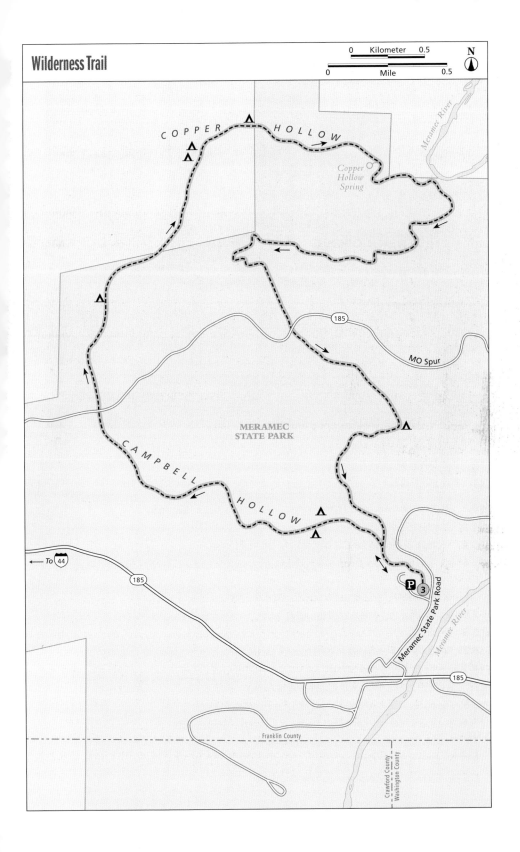

Wilderness Trail

0   Kilometer   0.5

0   Mile   0.5

N

COPPER HOLLOW

Copper
Hollow
Spring

Meramec River

185

MO Spur

MERAMEC
STATE PARK

CAMPBELL HOLLOW

← To 44

185

P 3

Meramec State Park Road

Meramec River

185

Franklin County

Crawford County
Washington County

Fall foliage on Wilderness Trail

Miles and Directions

0.0 From the Wilderness Trail parking area and trailhead, begin hiking north.

0.2 Reach the trail register and sign in.

0.4 The loop portion of the trail begins. Stay left (northwest).

0.6 The trail to the right leads to a backcountry campsite and another one at 0.7 mile to the left.

2.0 The trail crosses MO Spur Route 185. Continue north.

2.4 A connector trail enters from the right.

2.5 The trails to the left (west) go to backcountry campsites.

3.3 The trails to the left lead to backcountry campsites at 3.3, 3.4, and 3.7 miles.

4.3 Reach Copper Hollow Spring.

6.2 A connector trail comes in from the right (west).

6.8 The trail crosses MO Spur Route 185. Continue southeast.

7.4 The trail to the left (east) leads to the last backcountry campsite.

7.7 The trail crosses over Ridge Road. Continue south.

8.2 Reach the end of the loop.

8.6 Arrive back at the trailhead and parking area.

4 Pomme de Terre State Park: Indian Point Trail

The Indian Point Trail offers hikers a gentle stroll through a beautiful mixed-hardwood forest. The trail is highlighted by views of Pomme de Terre Lake from the rocky and rugged Indian Point. Hikers wishing to make a day of the hike can also enjoy a stop by the picnic area and beach that can be accessed from the trail.

Start: Indian Point Trail parking area in Pomme de Terre State Park
Distance: 3.1-mile loop
Hiking time: About 2 hours
Difficulty: Moderate due to length
Trail surface: Forested trail
Best season: Fall through spring
Other trail users: Hikers only
Canine compatibility: Leashed dogs permitted

Fees and permits: None
Schedule: Open year-round
Maps: USGS Sentinel; trail maps are available in the park office
Trail contacts: Pomme de Terre State Park, H.C. 77, Pittsburg, MO 65724; (417) 852-4291; www.mostateparks.com/park/pomme-de-terre-state-park

Finding the trailhead: From Springfield, Missouri, drive north on MO 13 for 26.2 miles. Turn right (north) onto MO 83 and drive 2.8 miles to Broadway Street. Turn right (east) onto Broadway Street and drive 0.9 mile before turning left (north) onto Missouri Highway D. Continue 13.7 miles on Missouri Highway D and then stay straight (north) onto MO 64. Drive 7 miles on MO 64 and then turn left (northwest) onto MO 64 Spur. Drive 1.9 miles into the park and to the parking area and trailhead on the left. GPS: N37 52.535' / W93 19.157'

The Hike

Pomme de Terre, literally translated as "apple of the earth," offers quite the recreational opportunity for those seeking it. The 734-acre state park offers an amazing array of terrain, some of the best that Missouri has to offer. The rugged hills of the Springfield Plateau mixed with glades, the Pomme de Terre River, and the Pomme de Terre Lake offer recreational possibilities for land lovers and water lovers alike. The 200-year-old post oaks and chinquapin oaks that grow in abundance here are classic indicators not only of the rocky terrain but also that this area was once an open woodland at the edge of the Great Plains.

Settlement of the area began in the 1830s. The Pomme de Terre River was actually the divider between white settlers and the natives. The spring-fed Pomme de Terre River was eventually dammed in the early 1960s by the US Army Corps of Engineers to create today's 7,800-acre Pomme de Terre Lake.

Hikers coming to Pomme de Terre State Park have a couple of options for a pleasant trekking experience. On the Hermitage side of the park, hikers can enjoy a more heavily wooded area that follows rocky bluffs along the lake's shoreline. On the Pittsburg side of the park, where Indian Point Trail is located, hikers will get to

Indian Point Trail

experience a trek through savanna woodland. Both sides offer the opportunity to see wild turkeys, deer, purple finches, and prairie warblers.

From the trailhead parking area, locate the Indian Point Trailhead kiosk at the northern end. Begin hiking north on the paved trail as it heads toward an outdoor amphitheater area and the pavement quickly ends and turns to a dirt surface. Continue hiking through the open woodland area, which is abundant with post oaks and chinquapin oaks. At 0.4 mile you will cross the park road and continue hiking north into the woodland area. After 0.6 mile you will come to a picnic area on the left (west) and make a sharp right turn east to continue on the Indian Point Trail. The trail continues for another 0.2 mile before reaching a restroom on the left (north), then a park road (left goes to a beach area), and then a connector trail. After crossing the park road, headed east, hikers will pass the red connector trail that offers a shorter hike. Continue hiking straight (northeast) to stay on the Indian Point Trail.

At 1.4 miles you'll reach the spur trail that leads out to Indian Point. Take a few moments to walk out onto the rugged and rocky peninsula and take in the views before returning to the trail, where you will now continue south on the trail. Once you've hiked through the woodland area and have taken in several views of the lake, you will

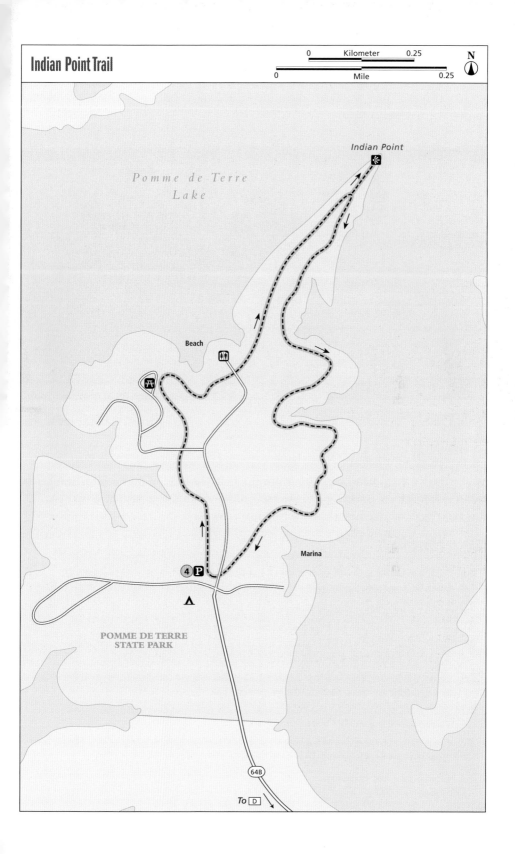

Indian Point Trail

0 | Kilometer | 0.25
0 | Mile | 0.25

N

Indian Point

Pomme de Terre Lake

Beach

Marina

4 P

POMME DE TERRE STATE PARK

64B

To D

Emily Tanner on Indian Point Trail

reach a bench at 2.7 miles that offers a nice place to rest while watching the folks down on the marina prep their boats. Return to the trail and hike southwest for 0.3 mile before reaching the southern end of the red connector trail. Continue hiking west past the connector trail and then across the park road. Return to the trailhead at 3.1 miles.

Miles and Directions

0.0 From the parking area, leave the trailhead kiosk and travel north on the Indian Point Trail, which is signed with blue arrows.

0.4 Cross the park road and continue north on the trail.

0.6 Reach a picnic area to the west. The trail turns sharply right (east).

0.8 Come to the Pittsburg Beach Area. Continue hiking east across the park road and quickly approach the red connector trail that heads south. Continue hiking straight (east).

1.4 Reach a spur trail that leads to Indian Point. After checking out the scenery, return to the trail and continue hiking south on the Indian Point Trail.

2.7 After hiking near the shore for a short stretch, you will come to a bench that has a good view of the marina.

3.0 Come to the southern end of the red connector trail that connects from the north and then cross the park road headed west.

3.1 Arrive back at the trailhead.

5 Ha Ha Tonka State Park: Devil's Kitchen Trail

Take a short hike through a state park that is well known for its numerous hiking trails. The Devil's Kitchen Trail offers many of the park's tourist sites all packed into one hike. A large sinkhole, glades, chert woodlands, a natural bridge, and views of the old castle ruins are just some of the sites that hikers can enjoy on this trek.

Start: Devil's Kitchen Trail parking area in Ha Ha Tonka State Park
Distance: 1.4-mile loop
Hiking time: About 1.5 hours
Difficulty: Easy to moderate due to length and moderate climbs
Trail surface: Rocky and forested trail
Best season: Fall through spring
Other trail users: Hikers only

Canine compatibility: Leashed dogs permitted
Fees and permits: None
Schedule: Open year-round
Maps: USGS Hahatonka; trail guide available at the visitor center
Trail contacts: Ha Ha Tonka State Park, 1491 State Road D, Camdenton, MO 65020; (573) 346-2986; www.mostateparks.com/park/ha-ha-tonka-state-park

Finding the trailhead: From Springfield, Missouri, drive 48.2 miles east on I-44 to exit 129. Turn left (northwest) onto MO 64 and drive 1.7 miles to MO 5. Turn right (north) onto MO 5 and drive 19 miles to Dry Hollow Road. Turn left (west) onto Dry Hollow Road and continue another 3.7 miles to State Highway D. Turn left onto State Highway D and then make an immediate left into the trailhead parking area. GPS: N37 58.423' / W92 45.749'

The Hike

The area that is now Ha Ha Tonka State Park was almost Missouri's first state park. In 1909 Missouri Governor Herbert Hadley proposed the idea but had his proposal rejected. So instead of becoming the first state park, the Ha Ha Tonka area had to wait until 1978 to become a state park. It is surprising considering that this area is known as "Missouri's karst showcase."

Features like a 70-foot-wide, 60-foot-long natural bridge, 150-foot-deep sinkholes, numerous caves, and even old castle ruins would seem to make this area a shoo-in for a state park. In 1903 Robert Snyder was so impressed with the area that he purchased over 5,000 acres here to build a European-style castle as a retreat for himself. Snyder began building his elaborate getaway in 1905 but was killed in one of the country's first automobile accidents only a year later. His sons finished the work, and the castle functioned as a hotel until 1942 when it was accidentally burned to the ground.

Hikers choosing to hike the Devil's Kitchen Trail will get a few glimpses of the old castle ruins and will have the option to visit the ruins via connecting trails if they choose. The 1.4-mile loop also takes hikers past some of the most amazing natural

Natural bridge on Devil's Kitchen Trail

features that the park has to offer its visitors. The park, which was carved from stone, will have you wanting more after hiking the Devil's Kitchen Trail.

From the trailhead parking area, begin hiking south on the gravel trail. The trail slowly rises up a moderate slope, and hikers will quickly approach Acorn Trail at 0.1 mile. Stay to the right and continue hiking south, following the brown blazes for the Devil's Kitchen Trail. The trail continues through an open woodland savanna and begins going downhill, reaching the Devil's Kitchen and Promenade by 0.4 mile. Continue hiking through the Kitchen and make your way up and across a large open-ing in the rocks. After stepping across the gap, make your way along the ledge that circles the sinkhole and eventually begin climbing out of the Kitchen. At 0.7 mile cross over Post Office Road and continue hiking northwest until you reach the Post Office Shelter Area at 0.9 mile. Turn right (north) to follow the footprints across State Highway D into the Spring Trail parking area and proceed down the stairs, where the Devil's Kitchen Trail and Spring Trail join each other briefly. At the bottom of the stairs, turn right (east) and continue to 1.1 miles to where the Spring Trail splits

JD Tanner on Devil's Kitchen Trail

Devil's Kitchen Trail

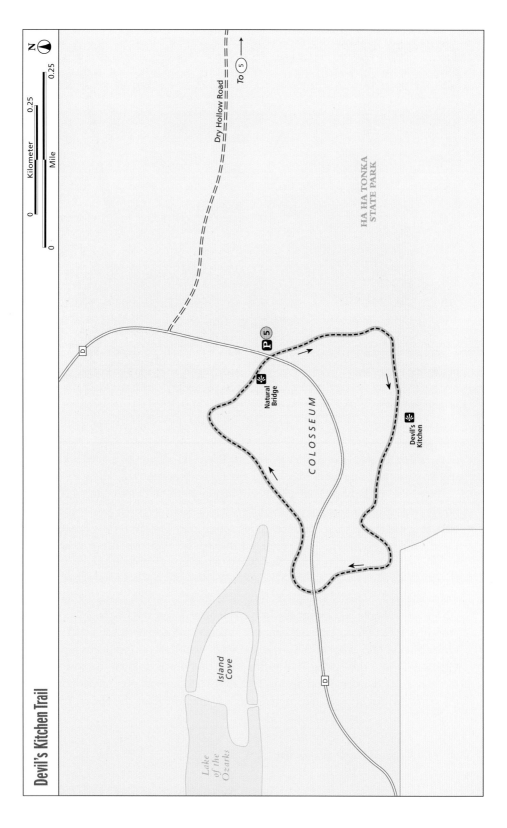

Lake of the Ozarks

Island Cove

COLOSSEUM

Natural Bridge

Devil's Kitchen

P 5

To 5 →

Dry Hollow Road

HA HA TONKA STATE PARK

D

D

N

0   Kilometer   0.25

0   Mile   0.25

away to the left (northwest) and the Devil's Kitchen Trail continues northeast. At 1.2 miles you'll turn right (northeast) to continue following the brown blazes, and shortly thereafter you'll take a sharp right (southeast) at a picnic area to cross over the natural bridge. The Colosseum sinkhole is to your left and right as you cross over the bridge. At 1.4 miles you'll cross over State Highway D again and return to the trailhead parking area.

Miles and Directions

- **0.0** From the parking area, locate the trailhead kiosk to the south and begin hiking south on the gravel trail up a moderate slope.
- **0.1** Acorn Trail splits to the left. Stay right (south) on the Devil's Kitchen Trail following the brown blazes.
- **0.4** After descending a hill into the Devil's Kitchen and Promenade, continue past a cave and take a big step across an opening in the rocks before walking along a ledge above the sinkhole.
- **0.7** Come to Post Office Road and cross the road to continue on the Devil's Kitchen Trail.
- **0.9** Turn right (north) at the Post Office Shelter Area and follow the footprints across State Highway D to continue down a set of stairs on the Devil's Kitchen Trail/Spring Trail.
- **1.0** At the bottom of the stairs, bear right (east) to stay on the Devil's Kitchen Trail.
- **1.1** The Spring Trail splits to the left (northwest). Continue northeast on the Devil's Kitchen Trail.
- **1.2** Turn right (northeast) to continue following the brown blazes, and soon after take another sharp right (southeast) to cross over the natural bridge.
- **1.4** Cross State Highway D and return to the trailhead parking area.

6 Clifty Creek Natural Area and Clifty Creek Conservation Area: Clifty Creek Trail

Clifty Creek Trail offers hikers a trip through one of Missouri's beautiful natural areas and conservation areas all in the same hike. The journey to the 40-foot-long natural bridge will offer hikers a chance to see some of the 450 plant species that have been recorded in the area. Plan to get your feet wet if you intend to hike the entire loop, especially during wet weather.

Start: Clifty Creek Trail parking area in Clifty Creek Conservation Area
Distance: 2.5-mile loop
Hiking time: About 2 hours
Difficulty: Moderate due to terrain
Trail surface: Forested trail
Best season: Any
Other trail users: Hikers only
Canine compatibility: Leashed dogs permitted
Fees and permits: None
Schedule: Open year-round
Maps: USGS Nagogami Lodge; trail map available at the trailhead
Trail contacts: MDC Central Regional Office, 1907 Hillcrest Dr., Columbia MO 65201; (573) 882-8388; http://mdc.mo.gov

Finding the trailhead: From Dixon, Missouri, drive 3.7 miles on MO 28 East. After 3.7 miles turn right (east) onto State Highway W. Continue on State Highway W for 3.4 miles to where the pavement ends and the road becomes gravel and changes into CR 511. Drive 1 mile on CR 511 to the parking area on the left (north) side of the road. GPS: N38 1.837' / W91 58.912'

The Hike

Clifty Creek became Missouri's first designated natural area in 1971. With the addition of the Clifty Creek Conservation Area in the 1980s, the two areas now combine for 486 acres of scenic dolomite cliffs. Hikers coming to the area can expect to see a typical Missouri hardwood forest filled with northern red oaks, white oaks, and mockernut hickories. Clifty Creek is also a popular spot for birders and animal lovers. Deer, squirrels, and turkeys can be seen in the area and, with the appropriate permits, can be hunted during hunting season. The only trail in the area takes hikers on a beautiful and scenic tour of some of the best that the land has to offer.

Locate the trailhead at the northeast corner of the parking lot and begin hiking west. After just 0.1 mile turn right to begin the loop portion of the trail and to begin a slow descent in Clifty Hollow. The trail continues a series of ups and downs until you reach the bottom of the hollow and Clifty Creek. At 1.0 mile hikers will reach a Clifty Creek crossing and the Clifty Creek Natural Bridge. A creek crossing will be necessary here to continue on the loop hike. Hikers who are not prepared to get their feet wet can simply turn around and return to the trailhead via the same route they just descended.

Clifty Creek Trail

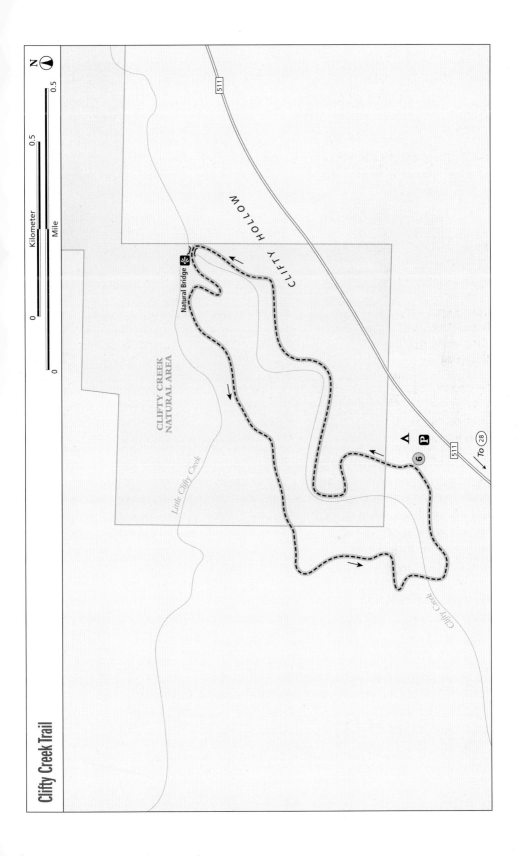

N

Kilometer
0   0.5   0.5

Mile
0   0.5

CLIFTY CREEK
NATURAL AREA

Little Clifty Creek

Natural Bridge

CLIFTY HOLLOW

511

Clifty Creek

6

P

511

To 28

Natural bridge on Clifty Creek Trail

After crossing Clifty Creek look for the trail to continue on the left (west) side of the natural bridge without going under the bridge. Once the trail is located, continue hiking up and out of the hollow. At 1.3 miles reach the top of the hollow and hike southwest along the rocky ridgeline as it parallels Clifty Creek and Clifty Hollow. The trail descends back down into the hollow at 2.2 miles and then crosses Clifty Creek again before climbing out of the hollow one more time toward the southeast. Reach the end of the loop portion of the hike at 2.4 miles and turn right (east) to return to the trailhead.

Miles and Directions

0.0 Begin hiking west from the parking area.

0.1 Turn right (north) to begin descending into Clifty Hollow.

1.0 Reach the Clifty Creek Natural Bridge and cross Clifty Creek to locate the trail to the left (west) of the bridge. Continue hiking southwest on the trail.

1.3 The trail reaches the north ridge of Clifty Hollow and continues southwest.

2.2 The trail descends back down in Clifty Hollow and crosses Clifty Creek again.

2.4 Reach the end of the loop portion of the trail.

2.5 Arrive back at the trailhead and parking area.

7 Taum Sauk Mountain State Park: Mina Sauk Falls Loop Trail/Ozark Trail to Devil's Tollgate

Taum Sauk Mountain State Park boasts both Missouri's highest point and Missouri's tallest waterfall. A visit to the highpoint first, then Mina Sauk Falls second, followed by a hike down to the Devil's Tollgate rock formation make this hike a nice little trifecta. It's an ideal hike following some wet weather, as the falls do not flow year-round.

Start: Taum Sauk Mountain parking area at Taum Sauk Mountain State Park
Distance: 5.1 miles out and back
Hiking time: About 3 hours
Difficulty: More challenging due to steep climb and rugged terrain
Trail surface: Forested path and rocky trail
Best season: Spring and fall
Other trail users: Hikers only

Canine compatibility: Leashed dogs permitted
Fees and permits: None
Schedule: Open year-round
Maps: USGS Ironton; Ozark Trail–Taum Sauk Section map available at the trailhead
Trail contacts: Johnson's Shut-Ins State Park, 148 Taum Sauk Trail, Middlebrook, MO 63656; (573) 546-2450; www.mostateparks.com/park/taum-sauk-mountain-state-park

Finding the trailhead: From Ironton, Missouri, drive 4.9 miles on MO 21 South and reach State Highway CC and the signed turn for Taum Sauk Mountain State Park. Turn right (west) onto State Highway CC and continue 3.6 miles to the parking area. GPS: N37 34.369' / W90 43.700'

The Hike

Located in the St. Francois Mountains, Taum Sauk Mountain State Park is one of the most rugged and beautiful locations in the state. Formed more than one billion years ago, this area was created when volcanic eruptions of hot ash settled and cooled to form rhyolite.

Traces of these mountains still remain, although they are now covered in hardwood forests of oak and hickory trees. The highest point in Missouri, Taum Sauk Mountain's elevation is 1,772 feet. This rugged day hike leads you past the highest point in the state and the tallest wet-weather waterfall in the state. You will also be on part of the longest trail in the state, the 350-mile-long Ozark Trail. The turnaround point for this hike is Devil's Tollgate, a hunk of volcanic rhyolite that stands over 30 feet tall.

Locate the Mina Sauk Falls Loop Trailhead at the southwest corner of the Taum Sauk Mountain parking area. Begin hiking southwest on the trail and reach a fork in the trail at 0.2 mile. Turning left takes you to the Missouri Highpoint; continue right (southwest) to a second fork at 0.3 mile that leads to a trailhead register. To the left is the Mina Sauk Falls Loop return trail. Stay right (southwest)

Mina Sauk Falls Loop/Ozark Trail to Devil's Tollgate

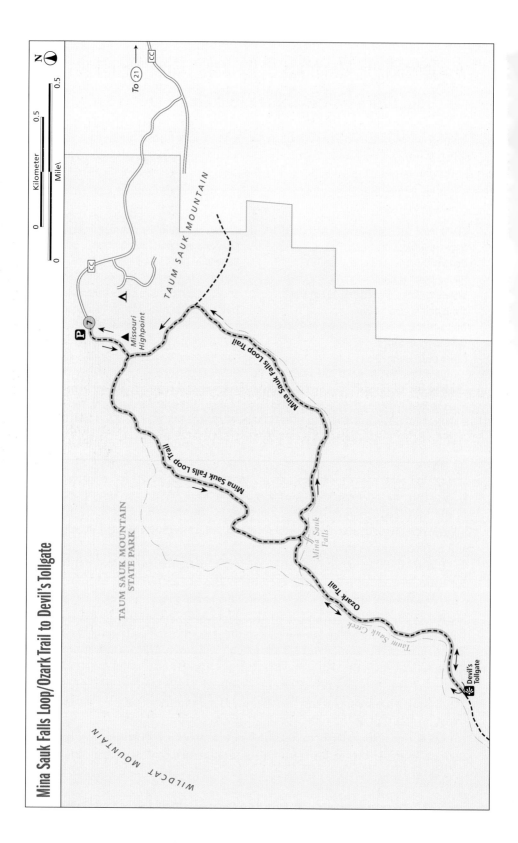

Mina Sauk Falls Loop Trailhead

as the trail becomes more rocky and rugged and descends slightly. Reach the junction of the Mina Sauk Falls Trail and Ozark Trail at 1.4 miles and bear right (southwest) onto the Ozark Trail.

The trail makes a steep descent down to the base of Mina Sauk Falls at 1.6 miles and continues on to the Devil's Tollgate at 2.4 miles. After a few pictures, return to the Mina Sauk Falls Loop Trail/Ozark Trail junction and turn right (east) to continue past the falls and keep hiking the loop. Reach a fork at 4.5 miles, where the Mina Sauk Falls Loop Trail leads to the left (northwest) and continues on to the trailhead register at 4.8 miles. Turn right (northeast) at the fork and reach another fork at 4.9 miles, where hikers will stay left (northeast) to return to the trailhead.

Miles and Directions

0.0 Begin hiking southeast from the Mina Sauk Falls Loop trailhead at Taum Sauk Mountain State Park.

0.2 Come to a fork in the trail and turn right (northeast). Left leads to the highest point in Missouri.

0.3 Reach a second fork and the trailhead register and stay right (northeast) again towards Mina Sauk Falls.

1.4 The Mina Sauk Falls Trail connects with the Ozark Trail. Left (east) leads to Mina Sauk Falls and continues on the loop. For now, turn right (west) onto the Ozark Trail towards the Devil's Tollgate and follow the OT white and green blazes.

1.6 Pass the base of Mina Sauk Falls.

2.4 Reach the Devil's Tollgate and turn around to return to Mina Sauk Falls.

3.8 Return to Mina Sauk Falls Loop Trail and Ozark Trail junction. Turn right (east) to continue on Mina Sauk Falls Trail and the Ozark Trail.

4.5 Reach the Ozark Trail and Mina Sauk Falls Loop Trail junction. Turn left (northwest) to complete the Mina Sauk Falls Loop Trail.

4.8 Return to the trailhead register and turn right (northeast).

4.9 Return to the first fork and stay left (northeast).

5.1 Arrive back at the trailhead.

8 Ozark Trail: Taum Sauk Mountain State Park to Johnson's Shut-Ins State Park

The Ozark Trail is Missouri's version of the Appalachian Trail. As of 2013, many sections of the trail are still under construction. The section of trail from Taum Sauk Mountain State Park to Johnson's Shut-Ins State Park is considered by many to be the best portion of the trail. This section offers rugged terrain, the highest point in the state, and beautiful scenery. Bring your swimsuit for this one and plan plenty of time to soak in the pools at Johnson's Shut-Ins.

Start: Taum Sauk Mountain parking area in Taum Sauk Mountain State Park
Distance: 26.4 miles out and back
Hiking time: About 2 to 3 days
Difficulty: More challenging due to rugged trail and length
Trail surface: Forested trail, rocky trail
Best season: Spring and fall
Other trail users: Hikers only

Canine compatibility: Leashed dogs permitted
Fees and permits: None
Schedule: Open year-round
Maps: USGS Ironton; Ozark Trail–Taum Sauk Section map available at the trailhead
Trail contacts: Johnson's Shut-Ins State Park, 148 Taum Sauk Trail, Middlebrook, MO 63656; (573) 546-2450; www.mostateparks.com/park/taum-sauk-mountain-state-park

Finding the trailhead: From Ironton, Missouri, drive 4.9 miles on MO 21 South. After 4.9 miles reach State Highway CC and the signed turn for Taum Sauk Mountain State Park. Turn right (west) onto State Highway CC and continue 3.6 miles to the parking area. GPS: N37 34.369' / W90 43.700'

The Hike

With over 350 miles of mostly linked trail sections, the Ozark Trail is the premier backpacking destination in Missouri. Future plans for the trail have it reaching from St. Louis to the Arkansas border and then linking with the Ozark Highland Trail in Arkansas to create a 700-mile trail and through-hiker paradise. Deer, turkeys, bobcats, bears, and bald eagles are just a few of the wild animals that you may encounter while hiking over the rugged hills of the Ozarks.

One of the most rugged sections of the trail is from Taum Sauk Mountain, at 1,773 feet, the highest point in the state, to Johnson's Shut-Ins State Park. In December 2005 a breach in the Taum Sauk Reservoir unleashed over one billion gallons of water, ripping trees and soil from the slopes of Proffit Mountain, devastating portions of Johnson's Shut-Ins State Park, and wiping out a large section of the Ozark Trail. In its wake the flood exposed a geological history few could imagine. Uncovering 1.4 billion years of the earth's history, geologists have found

both an ancient beach and mountain range. While signs of the devastating flood are still evident, most of the area has reopened and the lush, hardwood forest is beginning to take back much of the damaged area. In addition, several educational and interpretive exhibits have been added to the park to explain the amazing history uncovered by the reservoir breach.

The Ozark Trail from Taum Sauk Mountain to Johnson's Shut-Ins State Park is a great out-and-back backpacking trip, but it can also be done as a shuttle trip for hikers looking to crank out fewer miles. There are no designated campsites along this portion of the trail, but dispersed camping is allowed, or hikers could camp at the campground at Johnson's Shut-Ins State Park. If you choose to camp along the trail, please follow Leave No Trace guidelines on dispersed camping, if possible, by choosing a site that is on a durable surface and at least 200 feet from any water source or the trail.

Locate the Mina Sauk Falls Loop Trailhead at the southwest corner of the Taum Sauk Mountain parking area. Begin hiking southwest on the trail and reach a fork in the trail at 0.2 mile. Turning left takes you to the Missouri Highpoint; continue right (southwest) to a second fork at 0.3 mile. To the left is the Mina Sauk Falls Loop return trail. Stay right (southwest) as the trail becomes more rocky and rugged and descends slightly. Reach the junction of the Mina Sauk Falls Trail and Ozark Trail at 1.4 miles and bear right (southwest) onto the Ozark Trail.

The trail makes a steep descent down to the base of Mina Sauk Falls at 1.6 miles and continues on to the Devil's Tollgate at 2.4 miles. The trail climbs up above the valley floor and Taum Sauk Creek (perhaps to keep hikers higher in case of another reservoir disaster?). At 5.5 miles the trail makes a sharp left (south) turn and begins a steady ascent to a great view of the Ozarks and Taum Sauk Reservoir at 6.3 miles. Take in the views and continue north to Proffit Mountain.

At 10.7 miles hikers will pass an unnamed overlook to the left (south) and then a sign for Johnson's Shut-Ins State Park at 11.7 miles indicating that the park is 1.5 miles away. The Ozark Trail connects with the Scour Trail at 12.2 miles and continues west to 12.4 miles where hikers stay left on the Ozark Trail/Scour Trail. Keep left (north) again at the fork in the trail at 12.9 miles to stay on the Ozark Trail and reach the Scour Trail parking area at 13.2 miles. Once at Johnson's Shut-Ins State Park, hikers may want to take advantage of the natural pools that form along the East Fork of the Black River. If you are doing this as an out-and-back backpacking trip, return to Taum Sauk Mountain State Park via the same route.

Devil's Tollgate

Ozark Trail: Taum Sauk Mountain State Park to Johnson's Shut-Ins State Park

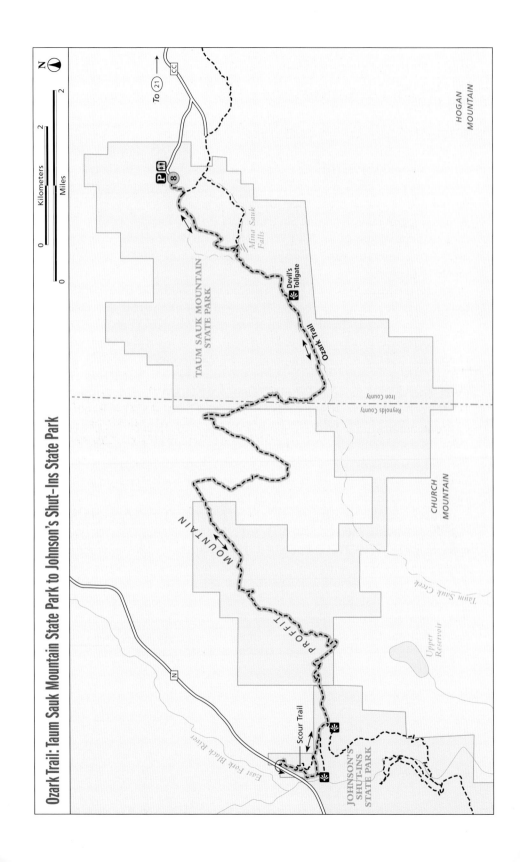

Miles and Directions

0.0 Begin hiking southwest from the Mina Sauk Falls Loop Trailhead at Taum Sauk Mountain State Park.

0.2 Come to a fork in the trail and turn right (northeast). Left takes you to the highest point in Missouri.

0.3 Reach a second fork and the trailhead register and stay right (northeast) again towards Mina Sauk Falls.

1.4 Mina Sauk Falls Trail connects with Ozark Trail. Left (east) leads to Mina Sauk Falls and continues on the loop. Turn right (west) onto the Ozark Trail towards the Devil's Tollgate and follow the OT white and green blazes.

1.6 Pass the base of Mina Sauk Falls.

2.4 Reach the Devil's Tollgate and continue hiking southwest.

5.5 The trail makes a sharp turn south and begins ascending.

6.3 The Taum Sauk Reservoir is viewable to the south.

10.7 Reach an unnamed overlook to the left (south).

11.7 Come to a sign for Johnson's Shut-Ins State Park (1.5 miles).

12.2 The Ozark Trail connects with the Scour Trail.

12.4 Stay left (west) on the Ozark Trail. The trail to the right is the Scour Trail loop.

12.9 Reach a fork and turn left (north). To the right is the Scour Trail loop.

13.2 Reach the Scour Trail parking area in Johnson's Shut-Ins State Park. Return to the Mina Sauk Falls Loop Trailhead at Taum Sauk Mountain State Park via the same route.

26.4 Arrive back at the Mina Sauk Falls Loop Trailhead at Taum Sauk Mountain State Park.

9 Washington State Park: Rockywood Trail

Known by many as Missouri's petroglyph showcase due to the largest known collection of carvings in the state, Washington State Park tends to be a memorable visit for many visitors. In addition to the 1,000-year-old petroglyphs, the park also offers rugged Ozark terrain for hiking enthusiasts. The Rockywood Trail is the longest trail offered by the park and includes the classic rolling and rugged terrain that you'd expect to find in the Ozarks.

Start: Thunderbird Lodge parking area and Rockywood Trailhead
Distance: 6.3-mile loop
Hiking time: About 3 to 4 hours
Difficulty: Moderate due to length of trail
Trail surface: Forested trail
Best season: Any
Other trail users: Hikers only
Canine compatibility: Leashed dogs permitted

Fees and permits: None
Schedule: Open year-round
Maps: USGS Tiff; trail map available at the Thunderbird Lodge
Trail contacts: Washington State Park, 13041 State Highway 104, De Soto, MO 63020; (636) 586-2995; http://mostateparks.com/park/washington-state-park

Finding the trailhead: From De Soto, Missouri, drive 10.5 miles west on MO 21 to MO 104. Turn right onto MO 104 and drive 1.5 miles on MO 104 before turning right into Washington State Park. Continue 1.1 miles to the Thunderbird Lodge parking area and Rockywood Trailhead. GPS: N38 5.126' / W90 41.061'

The Hike

Located near De Soto, Missouri, Washington State Park has a rich cultural and natural history. Several Native American rock carvings, or petroglyphs, have been found in the park, and unlike many of the rock carvings found in this part of the country, they have largely escaped vandalism. The petroglyphs are thought to have been created by the Middle Mississippi Culture around AD 1000.

The Rockywood Trail is the longest and most rugged trail in the park and is designed for both hiking and backpacking. Highlights of the trail include beautiful, open glades, rugged hardwood woodlands, and several scenic overlooks. A short detour from the trail will take you to one of the park's most popular interpretive areas, which contains over a dozen petroglyphs carved into slabs of limestone.

▶ What's the difference between a petroglyph and a pictograph? Both terms refer to rock art produced by Native Americans in the past. Petroglyphs are pictures or symbols that have been carved into the rock. Pictographs are painted onto the rock surface.

From the Thunderbird Lodge parking lot, locate the trailhead on the west side of the lodge. Begin hiking northwest behind the Thunderbird Lodge to a set

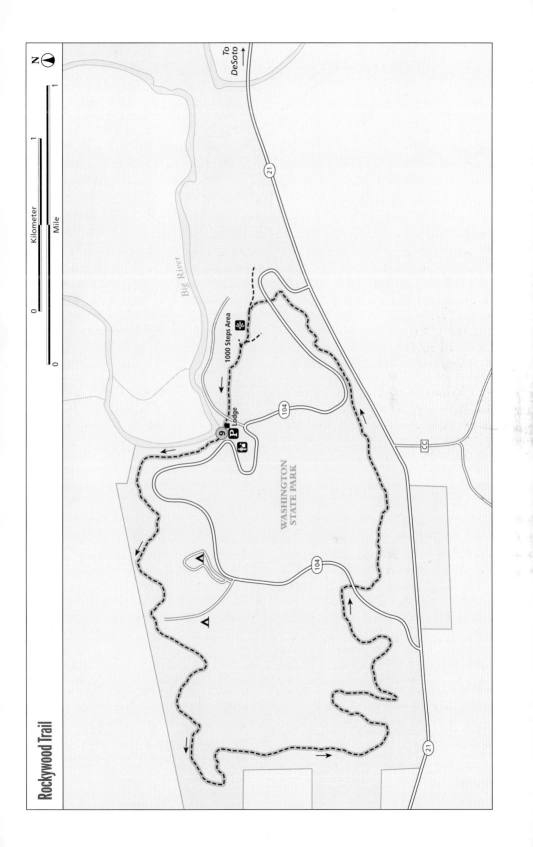

Rockywood Trail

of stairs leading up the bluff. The trail crosses Dugout Road at 0.5 mile and then reaches a trail junction at 0.8 mile. Continue hiking west; the trail to the left (south) is the Opossum Trail. At 2.2 miles the trail makes a sharp right and continues south.

As you are hiking east along the trail, you will cross SH 104 at 4.3 miles and then again at 5.7 miles. The Rockywood Trail joins the 1000 Steps Trail at 5.8 miles, where you will turn left (west) to continue down the 1000 Steps. When you reach the bottom of the Steps, turn left (west) at 6.1 miles and continue on to the east side of the parking area and end of the Rocky-wood Trail at 6.3 miles.

Miles and Directions

0.0 From the Thunderbird Lodge parking area and trailhead, begin hiking northwest on the Rockywood Trail.

0.5 Cross Dugout Road and continue hiking west.

0.8 Continue straight (west) on the Rockywood Trail. The Opossum Trail splits to the left (south).

2.2 The trail turns to the left (south).

4.3 The trail crosses SH 104. Continue south.

5.7 The trail crosses SH 104 again. Continue north.

5.8 Turn left (west) and descend the 1000 Steps Trail.

6.1 Turn left (west) at the bottom of the 1000 Steps.

6.3 Arrive back at the parking area.

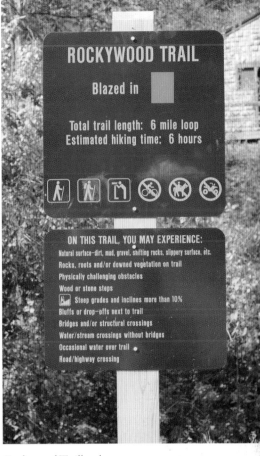

Rockywood Trailhead

Fall colors on Rockywood Trail

10 Sam A. Baker State Park: Mudlick Mountain Trail

This 7.8-mile loop trail climbs up and around Mudlick Mountain and offers overlooks of Big Creek and the surrounding Ozark hillsides and St. Francois Mountains, one of the oldest mountain ranges in North America. Fantastic views, historic old hiker shelters, and an optional short side trip to the top of Mudlick Mountain make this an excellent day trip. A small network of trails through the Mudlick Trail System provides several different hiking opportunities for shorter and longer hikes and backpacking trips.

Start: Mudlick Mountain Trail System parking area in Sam A. Baker State Park
Distance: 7.8-mile loop
Hiking time: About 4 to 5 hours
Difficulty: More challenging due to length and rugged terrain
Trail surface: Forested trail, dirt path
Best season: Best in fall from Sept to Nov for the fall foliage
Other trail users: Equestrians

Canine compatibility: Dogs permitted
Fees and permits: None
Schedule: Open year-round
Maps: USGS Brunot; trail map available at visitor center
Trail contacts: Sam A. Baker State Park, Route 1, Box 18150, Patterson, MO 63956-8768; (573) 856-4411 or (573) 856-4223; http://mostateparks.com/park/sam-baker-state-park

Finding the trailhead: From Patterson, Missouri, drive 1.1 miles east on MO 34. Turn left (north) onto MO 143. Continue 5.8 miles on MO 143 to the trailhead parking area on the left (west). GPS: N37 15.611' / W90 30.385'

The Hike

One of Missouri's oldest state parks, Sam A. Baker State Park has become an iconic family destination for many Missouri families. The park, established in 1926, typifies the classic Missouri state park experience, and each year new visitors adopt the tradition of enjoying family, friends, and nature in the beautiful hills of the Ozarks.

The park is named for former Missouri governor Samuel Aaron Baker, who advocated for its creation in the 1920s. When one witnesses the natural beauty of the area, it is easy to see why he hoped to preserve the area for generations to come. Like much of the Ozarks, dome-like knobs, valleys, exposed cliff bluffs, hardwood forests, and glades characterize the rugged landscape at Sam A. Baker State Park.

Similar to several of the early Missouri State Parks, this park offers visitors a unique outdoor experience on its 5,323 acres. Rustic cabins, a dining lodge, picnic shelters, and several hiking shelters showcase the craftsmanship of the Civilian Conservation Corps, which worked here during the 1930s. In addition to hiking, visitors here enjoy biking, horseback riding, camping, swimming, and backpacking. The park

Shelter on Mudlick Trail

provides access to both the St. Francis River and Big Creek, making canoeing, kayaking, and fishing popular pastimes in the park. Crappie, smallmouth bass, and catfish are just a few of the fish species that make their homes in these cool, clear waters.

The Mudlick Mountain Trail System begins just across the road from the stone dining lodge, which offers breakfast, lunch, and dinner from Memorial Day through Labor Day. This trail system traverses through the Mudlick Mountain Wild Area, one of the largest wilderness preserves in the Missouri state park system. Mudlick Mountain is also a Natural Area that provides hikers with a beautiful example of the effects of climatic conditions on mountain summit forests. Begin hiking northwest on the orange-blazed "hiking only" section of the Mudlick Trail. At 0.1 mile come to a wooden footbridge, which crosses a small drainage, and turn left (west) to cross the bridge and continue on the Mudlick Trail. Turning right (northeast) takes you to the Shut-Ins Trail. Look for white-tailed deer, turkey, and squirrels, which are commonly spotted throughout the park. Visitors may also see bobcats, raccoons, and opossums, more commonly sighted during evening hours.

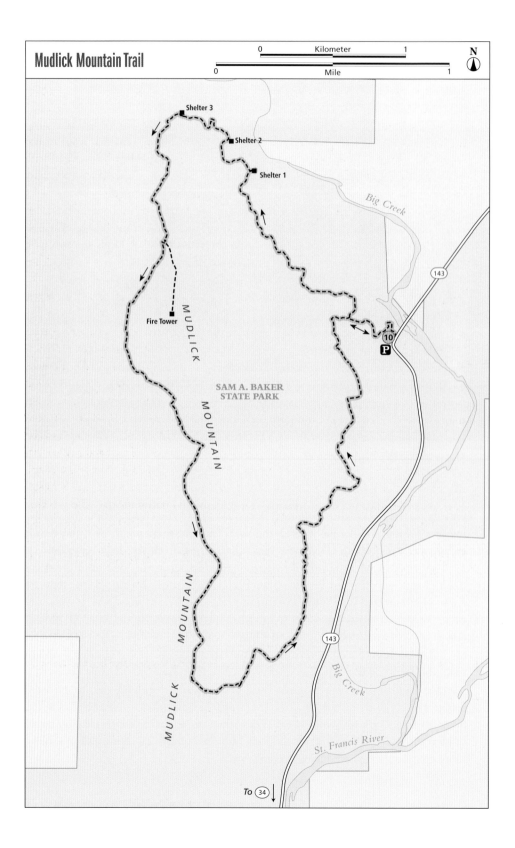

Mudlick Mountain Trail

Kilometer
0   1

Mile
0   1

N

Shelter 3

Shelter 2

Shelter 1

Big Creek

143

Fire Tower

MUDLICK

SAM A. BAKER
STATE PARK

MOUNTAIN

10
P

MUDLICK

MOUNTAIN

143

Big Creek

St. Francis River

To 34

At 0.4 mile come to a fork in the trail, stay right, and continue hiking north. Oak, hickory, sycamore, and cottonwood can all be seen while hiking along the trail. Also keep an eye out for the yellowwood tree, easily identified in the spring by its striking white, occasionally pink, blooms.

After hiking 1.4 miles you will reach the first of three hiking shelters. The hiking shelter is on the right (east) along with a blue-blazed hiking trail that leads to the Shut-Ins. Stay left (north) to continue hiking on the orange-blazed section of trail. The trail climbs north up the ridge to the next shelter at 1.7 miles and then the third shelter at 2.0 miles. Take in the views of Big Creek and then turn left (south) onto the yellow-blazed multiuse section of the Mudlick Trail that heads toward the fire tower and the summit of Mudlick Mountain. The last section of the hiking-only trail leaves the third shelter to the northwest and travels into Mudlick Hollow. A campsite is available in the hollow for those looking to overnight. Continue hiking south on the yellow-blazed portion of the Mudlick Trail to 2.7 miles. Stay right (southwest) to travel to the west of the summit and the fire tower. The trail that breaks off to the left (southeast) leads to the summit.

Once you've circled around the summit to the west, the trail crosses a service road at 3.5 miles. Continue hiking south across the road to pick the well-marked trail back up on the other side. At 3.7 miles turn right (south) toward Millers Ridge. Straight (east) leads to the Equestrian Day-Use Trailhead and left (northeast) takes you back up toward the fire tower and the mountain summit. Continue hiking south down the ridge as the trail crosses through a few openings and passes a small pond before you make a left (east) turn at 4.9 miles toward Camping Area #1. At 5.4 miles keep an eye out for the orange blazes of the "hiking only" section of trail and make a left (north) turn back onto this section. The trail becomes very rocky and rugged through this next stretch. Continue hiking north on the Mudlick Trail, a designated National Recreation Trail, to 6.5 miles, where the orange-blazed trail joins the yellow-blazed multiuse section of trail just briefly. Turn left (west) here and then right (north) at 6.6 miles to leave the multiuse section again.

At 7.4 miles reach the end of the loop section of the hike and turn right (southeast) to return to the trailhead and parking area at 7.8 miles.

Miles and Directions

0.0 Leave the Mudlick Mountain Trail System parking area, hiking northwest on the orange-blazed "hiking only" section of the trail.

0.1 Turn left (west) to cross the footbridge and continue on the Mudlick Mountain Trail. Going right leads to the Shut-Ins.

0.4 Stay right (north) on the Mudlick Mountain Trail; to the left (west) is your return trail.

1.4 Reach Hiking Shelter #1 on the right (east) and continue hiking north.

1.7 Come to Hiking Shelter #2 on the right (northeast) and continue hiking northwest.

2.0 Reach Hiking Shelter #3 on the right (north) and turn left (south) onto the yellow-blazed multiuse section of the trail toward the fire tower.

2.7 Stay right (southwest) on the Mudlick Trail; heading left (southeast) leads to the top of Mudlick Mountain and the fire tower.

3.5 Trail crosses a service road. Continue hiking south.

3.7 Turn right (south) toward Millers Ridge. Straight (east) leads to the Equestrian Day-Use area. Left (north) goes to the fire tower.

4.9 Turn left (east) toward Camping Area #1. Right (west) is extended hiking on the Mudlick Trail.

5.4 Watch closely for the orange-blazed "hiking only" section and turn left (north) onto the trail. Right (southeast) leads to Camping Area #1.

6.5 Turn left (west) onto the orange/yellow-blazed section of trail.

6.6 Turn right (north) onto the orange-blazed section of the Mudlick Trail.

7.4 The loop portion of the trail ends. Turn right (east) to return to the trailhead.

7.8 Arrive back at the Mudlick Mountain Trail System parking area and trailhead.

11 Pickle Springs Natural Area: Trail Through Time

A highlight of the Pickle Springs Natural Area, this short interpretive hike features towering limestone bluffs, breezy canyons, and several interesting sandstone rock formations. Visit in the early spring after wet weather to see the waterfall flowing. It is believed that the sandstone in this area is the remains of sandy beaches from a shallow ocean that existed here over 500 million years ago, hence the trail name Trail Through Time. Besides the beautiful rock formations, Pickle Springs Natural Area is also home to more than 250 species of plants.

Start: Trail Through Time parking area in Pickle Springs Natural Area
Distance: 2.0-mile loop
Hiking time: About 1 hour
Difficulty: Moderate due to modest climbs
Trail surface: Rock and forested trail
Best season: Any
Other trail users: Hikers only
Canine compatibility: Leashed dogs permitted

Fees and permits: None
Schedule: Open year-round
Maps: USGS Sprott; interpretive trail guide available at the information kiosk
Trail contacts: Pickle Springs Natural Area, 2302 County Park Dr., Cape Girardeau, MO 63701; (573) 290-5730; http://mdc.mo.gov/ discover-nature/places-go/natural-areas/ pickle-springs

Finding the trailhead: From St. Genevieve, Missouri, follow MO 32 West from the junction at I-55 past Hawn State Park to County Road AA. Turn left onto AA and drive about 1 mile to Dorlac Road. Turn left and follow Dorlac about 0.5 mile along the gravel road to the parking lot and trailhead located on the right. GPS: N37 48.083' / W90 18.087'

The Hike

Pickle Springs Natural Area received its name from Illinois settler William Pickles in the 1850s. As more has been learned about the area over the years, it has received more and more recognition. The area was designated a national natural landmark in 1974 and is a state natural area.

Researchers believe that mammoths once roamed the canyons, grazing on plants like northern white violets, orchids, and cinnamon ferns. All of these plants can still be found in Pickle Springs Natural Area. It tends to be the geology that keeps visitors coming back, though, and the Trail Through Time highlights some of the area's most unusual rock formations. The LaMotte sandstone has made its way from the bottom of ancient seas to expose rock formations not typically seen in Missouri. The sandstone, buried by layers upon layers of limestone, has been pushed back up to the surface as the Ozark Plateau has continued to rise.

The Trail Through Time is a 2.0-mile loop hike. The interpretive trail has been designed to lead hikers through all of the area's amazing sites. Hikers will have the

Double arch on Trail Through Time

opportunity to enjoy beautiful rock formations, cool box canyons, and a lush forest. The cool, moist canyon walls will provide nature lovers with numerous viewing opportunities. Seven species of ferns, more than forty species of liverworts, and several species of frogs all thrive in this amazing natural wonder. Some visitors will find that the 2.0-mile hike takes longer than an hour because of all the sights and sounds there are to take in.

From the parking area, begin hiking east on the obvious and well-maintained mulch trail. At 0.1 mile come to the information kiosk, which is stocked with trail maps and an interpretive pamphlet that corresponds with many of the sites along the trail. The loop begins at the information kiosk; turn left (north) to continue on the one-way trail. At 0.2 mile come to "the slot," a rock formation that is reminiscent of a slot canyon, only in miniature. Turn right (east), and cross through the tight canyon-like walls of LaMotte sandstone. Come to the more interesting rock formations, known as Cauliflower Rocks and Double Arch, at 0.4 mile. At 0.6 mile come to a wooden footbridge and continue northeast across Pickle Creek. Arrive at the bluff shelter known as Spirit Canyon at 1.0 mile; follow the trail as it curves to the right (west). Cross Pickle Creek again at 1.5 miles and continue west. At 1.7 miles come to Piney Glade, a sandstone glade near the top of the ridge, and follow the trail as it curves to the northwest. At 1.9 miles return to the information kiosk, turn left (west), and return to the parking area.

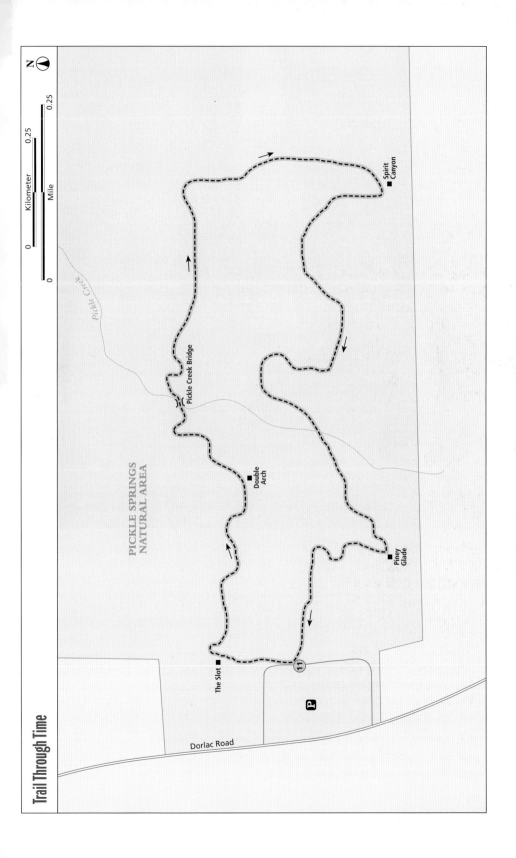

Trail Through Time

PICKLE SPRINGS
NATURAL AREA

Pickle Creek

Pickle Creek Bridge

Double Arch ■

The Slot ■

Piney Glade ■

Spirit Canyon ■

Dorlac Road

P

N

Kilometer
0   0.25

Mile
0   0.25

Trail Through Time

Miles and Directions

0.0 Begin hiking east on the obvious mulch trail.

0.1 Turn left (north) at the information kiosk.

0.2 Pass through "the slot."

0.4 Pass by Cauliflower Rock and through Double Arch.

0.6 Cross Pickle Creek and continue northeast.

1.0 Come to Spirit Canyon and begin heading west.

1.5 Cross Pickle Creek and continue west.

1.7 Come to Piney Glade and follow the trail as it curves to the northeast.

1.9 Return to the information kiosk and turn left (west).

2.0 Arrive back at the trailhead parking area.

12 Hawn State Park: Whispering Pines Trail–North Loop

A 6.5-mile loop through a mixed-hardwood and pine forest, the north loop of the Whispering Pines Trail offers a longer day trip for hikers looking to take in many of the sites in Hawn State Park. Several options exist to make your hike longer or shorter should you choose. An additional 4.0-mile southern loop can be used to extend your half-day hike to a full-day adventure.

Start: From the Whispering Pines Trailhead, located at Hawn State Park
Distance: 6.5-mile loop
Hiking time: About 4 hours
Difficulty: More challenging due to length and some steep climbs
Trail surface: Forested trail
Best season: Fall through spring
Other trail users: Hikers only

Canine compatibility: Leashed dogs permitted
Fees and permits: None
Schedule: Open year-round
Maps: USGS Coffman; trail maps available at the visitor center
Trail contacts: Hawn State Park, 12096 Park Dr., Ste. Genevieve, MO 63670; (573) 883-3603; www.mostateparks.com/park/hawn-state-park

Finding the trailhead: From St. Genevieve, Missouri, follow MO 32 West from the junction at I-55 for 11.3 miles to MO 144. Turn left onto MO 144 and follow the road for 2.9 miles to the park entrance. At the stop sign turn left onto Park Drive and continue 1.1 miles to a fork. Stay right at the fork and drive 0.1 mile to the parking area and trailhead on the left. GPS: N37 49.760' / W90 13.811'

The Hike

Many of the visitors who come to Hawn State Park believe it to be the loveliest park in Missouri. The 4,953-acre park is located in the eastern Ozark Mountains and is home to the 2,880-acre Whispering Pine Wild Area and Pickle Creek, a state natural area. The park was acquired by the state in 1955.

The area is believed to have been part of a large, sandy floodplain around 600 million years ago, which stretched as far north as Canada. Through cycles of uplift and erosion, the sandstone cliffs and bluffs are what remain. Today, hikers can enjoy rich shortleaf pine forests, mixed oak and maple trees, and plenty of flowering dogwoods. The park is also popular with rock hounds and birders.

The Whispering Pines North Trail is a 6.5-mile loop hike. On a windy day, you will learn why the trail is called the Whispering Pines Trail. Many people say it sounds like the pine trees are actually whispering to you as the wind blows through them. For an extended hike or even a short, overnight backpacking trip, the north loop can be combined with the south loop for a 10.0-mile hike.

From the parking area, locate the Whispering Pines Trail to the south. There is a sign marking the trail at the trailhead, and hikers are encouraged to sign in at the trailhead register. Cross the wooden footbridge and continue hiking south to cross a

View from Whispering Pines Trail

second wooden footbridge at 0.1 mile. Turn right here and follow the red directional arrow southwest. At 0.3 mile come to a fork in the trail and stay right (southwest) to stay on the Whispering Pines Trail—North Loop. Wade across the babbling Pickle Creek at 1.0 mile and turn left (west). Come to Connector Trail #1, which connects to the White Oaks Trail, at 1.3 miles, stay left, and continue hiking southwest on the Whispering Pines Trail—North Loop. At 1.8 miles come to Connector Trail #2, which also connects to the White Oaks Trail, stay left, and continue southwest.

At 3.2 miles come to Connector Trail #3 on the left (north) side of the trail, which leads to a primitive camping area and can be used to shorten this hike as it eventually leads to the trailhead parking area. Stay right (east) to continue on the Whispering Pines Trail—North Loop. At 3.7 miles come to the junction of the Whispering Pines Trail—North Loop and the Whispering Pines Trail—South Loop. Stay to the left (northeast) to continue on the north loop. At 3.8 miles come to a second junction with the south loop, again stay left (north) to continue on the north loop, and return to the trailhead. Come to Pickle Creek at 5.4 miles and follow the trail as it turns to the left (southwest). At 6.4 miles return to the footbridge, turn right (north) to cross the bridge, and return to the trailhead parking area.

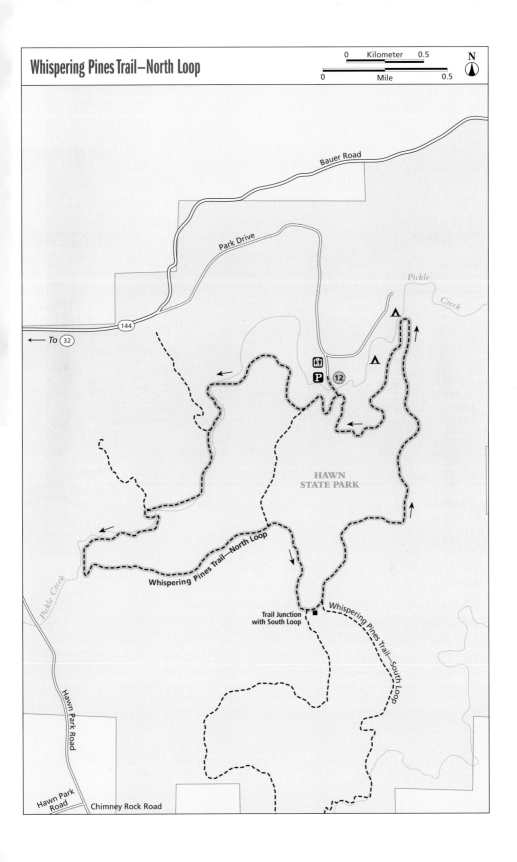

Whispering Pines Trail—North Loop

Kilometer
0   0.5

Mile
0   0.5

N

Bauer Road

Park Drive

Pickle Creek

144

← To 32

🚻
🅿️ 12

△

△

HAWN
STATE PARK

Whispering Pines Trail—North Loop

Pickle Creek

Trail Junction
with South Loop

Whispering Pines Trail—South Loop

Hawn Park
Road

Hawn Park
Road   Chimney Rock Road

Pickle Creek

Miles and Directions

0.0 Begin hiking south, crossing a wooden footbridge.

0.1 Cross a second wooden footbridge and turn right (southwest).

0.3 Come to a fork in the trail, stay right, and continue southwest.

1.0 Cross Pickle Creek and turn left (west).

1.3 Avoid Connector Trail #1.

1.8 Avoid Connector Trail #2.

3.2 Avoid Connector Trail # 3 and continue east.

3.7 Avoid the Whispering Pines Trail—South Loop and continue northeast.

3.8 Stay left (north) at the second junction with the Whispering Pines Trail—South Loop.

5.4 Come to Pickle Creek. The trail turns to the left (southwest).

6.4 Return to the wooden footbridge, turn right (north) to cross the bridge, and return to the trailhead parking area.

6.5 Arrive back at the trailhead.

13 Amidon Memorial Conservation Area: Cedar Glade Trail

Amidon Memorial Conservation Area offers one of the only granite shut-ins in Missouri. The pink granite rocks make the area a popular swimming hole during the summer, and the 1.0-mile Cedar Glade Trail explores some of the more interesting features in the area.

Start: From the Amidon Memorial Conservation Area parking area
Distance: 1.0-mile loop
Hiking time: About 30 minutes (plan on spending more time if you wish to explore the shut-ins)
Difficulty: Easy
Trail surface: Forested path
Best season: Any
Other trail users: Hikers only
Canine compatibility: Leashed dogs permitted

Fees and permits: None
Schedule: Open year-round; conservation areas are closed from 10 p.m. to 4 a.m. except for authorized camping, fishing, and hunting activities
Maps: USGS Fredericktown
Trail contacts: Missouri Department of Conservation, Southeast Regional Office, 2302 County Park Dr., Cape Girardeau, MO 63701; (573) 290-5730; http://mdc.mo.gov

Finding the trailhead: From Fredericktown, Missouri, drive 1.9 miles east on MO 72. After 1.9 miles turn left (northeast) onto State Highway J. Continue on J for 4.4 miles to State Highway W. Turn right (south) onto W and drive 1.2 miles to CR 208. Turn left (east) onto CR 208 and continue 1.1 miles to CR 253. Turn left (north) onto CR 253 and drive 0.8 mile to the parking area on the right. GPS: N37 34.141' / W90 9.3'

The Hike

Located in Bollinger and Madison Counties, the 1,632-acre Amidon Memorial Conservation Area is a fantastic destination almost any time of year. Locally the area is often referred to as either Pink Rocks or Hahns Mill. The first nickname obviously refers to the main geological feature in the area, while Hahns Mill refers to the area's history as a grain mill in the late 1800s.

The crystal-clear waters of the Castor River flow through the incredibly pink granite shut-ins, forming natural slides, waterfalls, and swimming holes. Visit at sunset to see a picturesque scene as the granite glows in shades of pinks, oranges, and purples. The rocks radiate warmth after baking in the sun all day, making it an enjoyable destination even on cool days.

The mostly hardwood forest is dominated by oak, hickory, and maple, although you will also see white ash, black gum, and sassafras. Growing along the steep banks of the Castor River, shortleaf pine and eastern red cedar punctuate the skyline. Look for prickly pear cactus and the purple blooms of wild hyacinths as you cross through glade restoration area.

Cedar Glade Trail

0   Kilometer   0.25

0   Mile   0.25

N

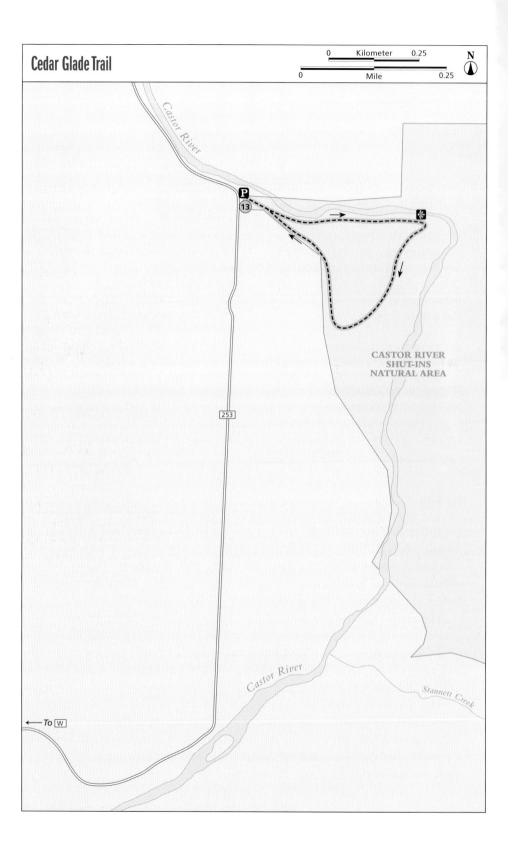

Castor River

P
13

CASTOR RIVER
SHUT-INS
NATURAL AREA

253

Castor River

Stannett Creek

← To W

Shut-ins at Amidon Memorial Conservation Area

The 1.0-mile Cedar Glade Trail is a great place to begin your exploration of this area. The natural-surface trail begins on the eastern side of the parking area and traverses a field that provides a food source for wildlife in the area.

At 0.1 mile the trail forks. Stay left (east) as the trail winds through the hardwood forest until it reaches the banks of the Castor River and the shut-ins at 0.3 mile. Here you will want to leave the trail to explore the rocks, wade, swim, picnic, or just enjoy the natural beauty of the area. After taking in the sights, return to the trail as it parallels the river for a short time before turning right (southwest) into the forest. At 0.7 mile cross two footbridges.

At 0.85 mile come to the end of the loop and turn left (west) to return to the trailhead and parking area.

Miles and Directions

0.0 Begin hiking east on the natural-surface trail.

0.1 At the fork in the trail, continue left (east).

0.3 Reach the shut-ins area.

0.7 Cross two footbridges.

0.8 Come to the end of the loop and turn left (west).

1.0 Arrive back at the trailhead and parking area.

14 Trail of Tears State Park: Sheppard Point Trail

This exceptional day hike offers steep inclines and scenic ridgetop views of the Mississippi River. Located in the Trail of Tears State Park just outside of Cape Girardeau, Missouri, this hike is perfect for nature lovers and the park is a great place to catch up on the history of the Trail of Tears.

Start: From the Sheppard Point Trail parking area at Trail of Tears State Park
Distance: 3.1-mile lollipop
Hiking time: About 2 to 2.5 hours
Difficulty: Moderate due to several steep climbs
Trail surface: Forested trail
Best season: Any
Other trail users: Hikers only

Canine compatibility: Leashed dogs permitted
Fees and permits: None
Schedule: Open year-round
Maps: USGS Ware
Trail contacts: Trail of Tears State Park, 429 Moccasin Springs Rd., Jackson, MO 63755; (573) 334-1711; www.mostateparks.com/park/trail-tears-state-park

Finding the trailhead: From Fruitland, Missouri, drive east on US 61 North/High Street for 1.1 miles to MO 177. Turn right (east) onto MO 177 and continue 7.4 miles to a stop sign. Turn right (south) to stay on MO 177 and drive 4.1 miles to the park entrance. Turn left (northeast) onto Moccasin Springs Road and drive 0.3 mile before passing the visitor center on the left. Continue another 0.9 mile to the Greensferry Shelter/Sheppard Point Trailhead on the right. GPS: N37 26.697' / W89 28.007'

The Hike

Trail of Tears State Park offers some of the best day hikes in southeast Missouri. Rich in both natural and cultural history, the park makes an excellent weekend destination and is a relatively short distance from St. Louis thanks to the direct route that I-55 offers.

The park's name hints at one of America's darkest chapters. The Indian Removal Act of 1830 set the stage for the relocation of Native Americans living east of the Mississippi River. Many tribes were affected by the act, including members of the Cherokee, Choctaw, Chickasaw, Creek, and Seminole nations. Trail of Tears State Park honors the relocation of the Cherokee. During the winter of 1838–39, more than 16,000 Cherokee were forced to relocate from their homelands in and around western North Carolina to Indian Territory, which is in present-day Oklahoma. The 1,000-mile journey took the lives of more than 4,000 people along the way and came to be known as the Trail of Tears. The park's visitor center offers an excellent interpretation of this tragic event and is well worth a visit.

Positioned on the banks of the mighty Mississippi River, this state park is a prime location for viewing migrating waterfowl, including several species of ducks. The Sheppard Point Trail is also a prime location to spot eagles, particularly in winter.

White-tailed deer

The Sheppard Point Trail is located just west of the Greensferry Shelter on Moc-casin Springs Road. From the trailhead, begin hiking southeast on the obvious and well-marked dirt path. The trail quickly begins to ascend a moderately steep ridge through the hardwood woodland of mostly oak and hickory trees. After hiking 0.9 mile you will come to the beginning of the loop portion of the hike, marked by a wooden bench, which many hikers will use as they catch their breath after the long incline. From here, continue hiking north on the left fork of the trail. After about 100 yards you may notice a faint path that branches to the right (east). Ignore this path, which runs out after a few hundred yards, and continue on the more obvious trail as it heads due north toward the Mississippi River.

At 1.2 miles you'll come to a second wooden bench, at which point the trail makes a drastic turn to the south, descending the ridge. Look for beech, poplar, and magnolia trees as you hike through this valley before climbing another steep ridge that takes you to Sheppard Point at 1.7 miles from the trailhead. This bluff offers one of the best views in the park. Keep an eye on both the sky and the ground at this point, as we have spotted both eagles and timber rattlesnakes on this portion of the

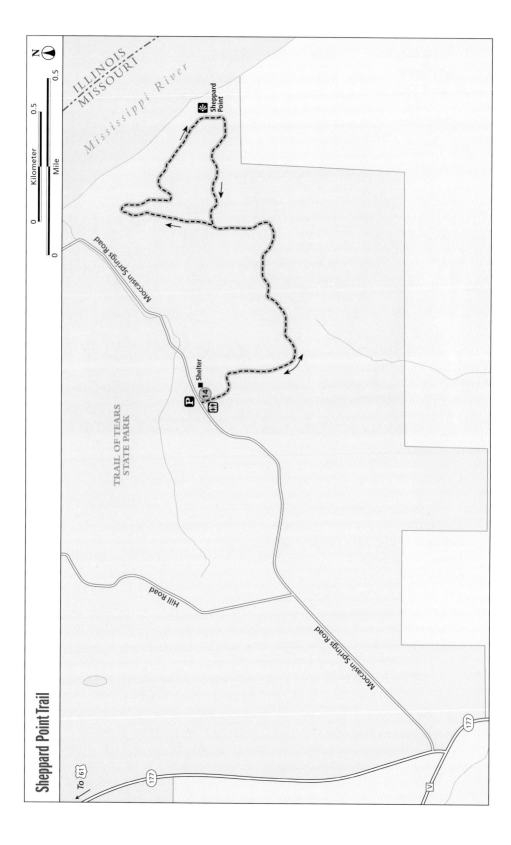

Sheppard Point Trail

Mississippi River

ILLINOIS
MISSOURI

Sheppard
Point

Moccasin Springs Road

Shelter

14

P

TRAIL OF TEARS
STATE PARK

Hill Road

Moccasin Springs Road

To 61

177

177

V

N

Kilometer

Mile

0   0.5

0   0.5

trail. After Sheppard Point the trail makes a sharp turn to the west and descends the ridge. After about 0.25 mile you will hike into a valley and then make your final steep climb to finish the loop portion of the hike.

At 2.2 miles finish the loop portion of the hike and turn south (left), descending the ridge back to the parking area. Return to the trailhead and parking area at 3.1 miles.

Miles and Directions

0.0 From the trailhead register, begin hiking southeast.

0.9 Come to the beginning of the loop portion of the hike (bench); continue straight (north). Soon you will come to a faint trail that branches to the right (east)—avoid this trail and continue north on the more obvious trail.

1.2 Come to a second bench and scenic overlook. The trail makes a sharp turn to the south and descends the ridge.

1.7 Reach Sheppard Point (bench and overlook).

2.2 Reach the end of the loop. Stay left (south) and return to the trailhead via the same route.

3.1 Arrive at the trailhead.

15 Blue Spring Natural Area: Blue Springs Trail

According to local legend, the people of the Osage tribe called this spring the "Spring of the Summer Sky." This trail follows the banks of the Current River to the deepest spring in the state of Missouri.

Start: From the trailhead at the Powder Mill Campground in the Blue Spring Natural Area
Distance: 3.0 miles out and back
Hiking time: About 2 hours
Difficulty: Easy
Trail surface: Forested trail
Best season: Any
Other trail users: Hikers only
Canine compatibility: Leashed dogs permitted

Fees and permits: None
Schedule: Open year-round
Maps: USGS Eminence
Trail contacts: Missouri Department of Conservation—Southeast Regional Office, 2302 County Park Dr., Cape Girardeau 63701; (573) 290-5730; http://mdc.mo.gov/discover-nature/places-go/natural-areas/blue-spring

Finding the trailhead: From the small town of Eminence, Missouri, drive east on MO 106 for 13.4 miles. Turn right (south) onto CR 531 toward the Powder Mill Campground and continue 0.6 mile to the parking area on the left (east). GPS: N37 10.935' / W91 10.477'

The Hike

next to current ~10 sites.

This easy day hike will take you to one of the most beautiful springs in the United States. The turquoise-hued waters of the aptly named Blue Spring make for a wonderful hike destination for those lucky enough to visit this part of the Ozarks. While slightly longer than the traditional path to Blue Spring, this out-and-back trail follows the banks of the Current River and gives hikers the opportunity to enjoy the area's diverse flora and fauna.

Blue Spring has an average daily flow of around ninety million gallons, making it the sixth-largest spring in Missouri. This impressive flow is responsible for the formation of underground caves and water passages as the rushing water dissolves limestone and dolomite. At 300 feet, it does hold the record for being the deepest spring in the state, and it is certainly one of the most visually stunning springs you are ever likely to see.

The spring's color is in part a result of its extreme depth, as well as minerals, such as limestone and dolomite, and organic matter that are suspended in the water.

Blue Spring offers a nice hike any time of the year, although spring and fall are particularly pleasant. Spring hikers will be treated to displays of Ozark wildflowers that grow along the river, spring, and steep bluffs that surround the spring. Those visiting in fall will be impressed by the contrast of the water with the fiery display of orange, red, and yellow leaves of the turning trees. Other factors such as cloud cover and rainfall can temporarily affect the water's color, but it is always stunning.

146 mi for Sptd.

~2 ½ hrs

Blue Spring ▶

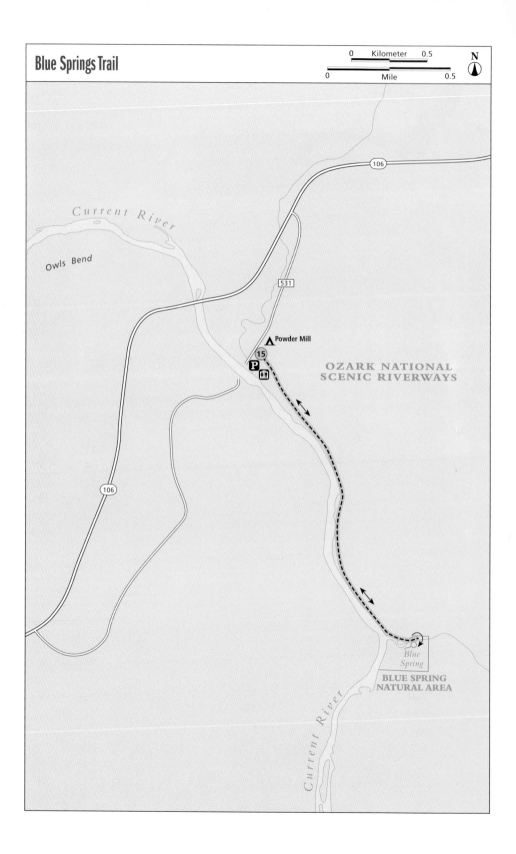

Blue Springs Trail

0   Kilometer   0.5
0   Mile   0.5

N

Current River

Owls Bend

106

531

Powder Mill

15

OZARK NATIONAL
SCENIC RIVERWAYS

106

Blue
Spring

BLUE SPRING
NATURAL AREA

Current River

Blue Spring Natural Area

While completely surrounded by National Park Service land, the 17-acre Blue Spring Natural Area is owned by the Missouri Department of Conservation. Both agencies provide interpretive information about the area.

From the trailhead at the Powder Mill Campground, begin hiking southeast on the obvious dirt path through bottomland woodland. After a short distance the trail begins to parallel the Current River and basically follows the river until the trail reaches Blue Spring Overlook. Look for trees such as sycamore, box elder, and river birch, all of which can withstand periodic flooding.

At 0.4 mile cross a wooden footbridge over a small drainage and continue hiking southeast along the banks of the Current River, which is part of the Ozark National Scenic Riverways and managed by the National Park Service. Come to a rest bench at 0.65 mile.

At 1.2 miles come to a fork in the trail; stay right (southeast) to continue along the Current River toward Blue Spring. At 1.5 miles reach Blue Spring Overlook. Return to the trailhead and parking area at Powder Mill Campground via the same route.

Miles and Directions

0.0 Start at the Powder Mill Campground parking area and begin hiking southeast on the obvious dirt trail.

0.4 Cross a footbridge and continue southeast.

1.2 Stay right (southeast) at the fork.

1.5 Reach Blue Spring Overlook. Return the way you came.

3.0 Arrive back at Powder Mill Campground.

16 Ozark Trail: Klepzig Mill to Rocky Falls

This interesting and beautiful section of the Ozark Trail begins at the historic Klepzig Mill and shut-ins and ends at the equally impressive Rocky Falls. Hikers taking on this journey should be prepared to take a dip and cool off at the Rocky Falls, a popular place for tourists and locals to relax during the hot summer months.

Start: From the Klepzig Mill parking area
Distance: 6.2 miles out and back
Hiking time: About 4 hours
Difficulty: Moderate due to length and terrain
Trail surface: Forested trail; short section along road
Best season: Fall through spring
Other trail users: Hikers only

Canine compatibility: Leashed dogs permitted
Fees and permits: None
Schedule: Open year-round
Maps: USGS Stegall Mountain
Trail contacts: Ozark Trail Association, 406 W. High St., Potosi, MO 63664; (573) 436-0540; ozarktrail.com

Finding the trailhead: From Eminence, Missouri, drive east on MO 106 for 7 miles. Turn right (south) onto State Route H and continue driving for 4 miles. Turn left (east) onto State Route NN and drive 4.2 miles until you reach Shannon CR 522, which forks to the left (north). Drive 1.3 miles to the trailhead parking area on the left (south). GPS: N37 7.581' / W91 11.937'

The Hike

This section of the Ozark Trail makes an excellent day hike for those looking to explore the exceptional beauty of the Ozarks. The trail begins near Klepzig Mill and shut-ins. On the National Register of Historic Places, the small turbine mill was constructed in 1928 by Walter Klepzig. There is also a series of small shut-ins in this area. Although smaller in size than other shut-ins found in the region, such as Johnson's Shut-Ins, the area is well worth a visit any time of year.

At the southern end of this trail, where you will leave your vehicle, lies Rocky Falls, an impressive 40-foot waterfall that cascades over a series of rhyolite steps. During hot weather you will likely find the area crowded with swimmers. While it is an excellent swimming hole, if you are looking for solitude, visit during cooler weather.

From the trailhead, begin hiking south on the rocky doubletrack path, following the green-and-white Ozark Trail markers. The trail shortly returns to the banks of

Mushroom growing on Ozark Trail

Klepzig Mill, built in 1928

Rocky Creek, which provides amazing scenery and offers ample opportunities for wading in the cool, clear creek.

At 0.9 mile come to some shut-ins and enjoy the scenery as you pass between Mill and Buzzard Mountains. Pay close attention as the trail climbs a small hill at 1.0 mile—it is easy to miss. This small doubletrack trail reaches State Road NN at 1.2 miles. Turn right (southwest) and walk along the side of the road for a short distance. Cross Rocky Creek again at 1.6 miles and look for the green-and-white Ozark Trail markers on the left (south) side of the road.

Leave State Road NN and hike south on the Ozark Trail, passing through a small grove of eastern red cedars and coming to a grassy clearing at 1.7 miles. Here the scenery is quite different from the mostly hardwood forest you just left. Count on seeing a variety of wildflowers here much of the year.

At 2.6 miles cross the creek and continue on the trail to a trail intersection at 2.7 miles. Turn right (west) here and follow the grassy path to Rocky Falls. Reach the Rocky Falls parking area at 3.1 miles. A paved walkway leads to the falls. Return to Klepzig Mill via the same route. At 6.2 miles arrive back at the Klepzig Mill and the parking area.

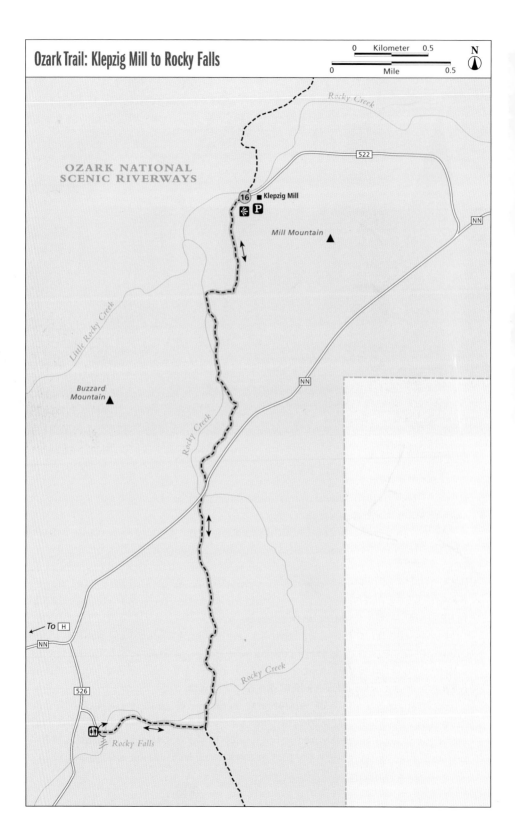

0   Kilometer   0.5

N

0   Mile   0.5

Rocky Creek

522

OZARK NATIONAL
SCENIC RIVERWAYS

NN

16   ■ Klepzig Mill

P

Mill Mountain   ▲

Little Rocky Creek

Buzzard
Mountain   ▲

Rocky Creek

NN

To H

NN

526

Rocky Creek

Rocky Falls

Rocky Falls in summer

Miles and Directions

0.0 Start at the small parking area at Klepzig Mill and begin hiking south on the rocky doubletrack.

0.9 Reach the shut-ins.

1.0 The trail climbs a small hill.

1.2 Come to State Road NN, turn right (southwest), and follow the road.

1.6 Cross Rocky Creek and turn left (south) onto the Ozark Trail.

1.7 Come to a grassy clearing.

2.6 Cross a creek.

2.7 Come to a spur trail to Rocky Falls. Turn right (west) onto a spur trail.

3.1 Arrive at Rocky Falls. Return to Klepzig Mill via the same route.

6.2 Arrive back at Klepzig Mill parking area.

17 Ruth and Paul Henning Conservation Area: Homesteaders Trail

Located on the west side of Branson, Missouri, is the Ruth and Paul Henning Conservation Area. This area used to be a state forest but is now a conservation area and offers visitors an opportunity to witness the natural and cultural significance of the area.

Start: From the Homesteaders Trailhead parking lot
Distance: 3.6-mile loop
Hiking time: About 2 to 3 hours
Difficulty: Moderate due to rocky terrain
Trail surface: Forested trail, rocky path
Best season: Any
Other trail users: Hikers only
Canine compatibility: Leashed dogs permitted
Fees and permits: None

Schedule: Open year-round
Maps: USFS Garber; self-guided-trail booklet available at the Springfield Conservation Nature Center, Shepherd of the Hills Fish Hatchery, and Branson Forestry Office
Trail contacts: Missouri Department of Conservation, Branson Forestry Office, 226 Claremont Dr., Branson, MO 65616; (417) 334-3324; http://mdc.mo.gov

Finding the trailhead: From Springfield, Missouri, drive south on US 65 for 35 miles to MO 465. Turn right onto MO 465 and drive 2.5 miles before turning left (south) onto Sycamore Church Road. Drive 3.8 miles on Sycamore Church Road to the parking area on the left. GPS: N36 41.017' / W93 17.292'

The Hike

The 1,534-acre Ruth and Paul Henning Conservation Area is located in the White River Hills. The White River Hills are located on the west side of Branson and are known for their steepness, oak–hickory forests, and dolomite glades. Glades are small, desertlike areas that break up the mostly forested landscape here. These delicate, sunny glades are home to plants and animals not commonly associated with the Midwest. Eastern collared lizards, scorpions, tarantulas, and roadrunners have all found homes in these Ozark glades. When glades occur on ridges or knobs, they are often called balds. These areas play an important role in local folk history. They served as rendezvous points for the vigilante groups known as the Bald Knobbers after the Civil War.

The area is named for Ruth and Paul Henning, who donated much of the land for the conservation area. Paul Henning, a Missouri native, was the creator of several popular television shows, including *The Beverly Hillbillies, Petticoat Junction,* and *Green Acres.*

JD on Henning Homesteaders Trail ▶

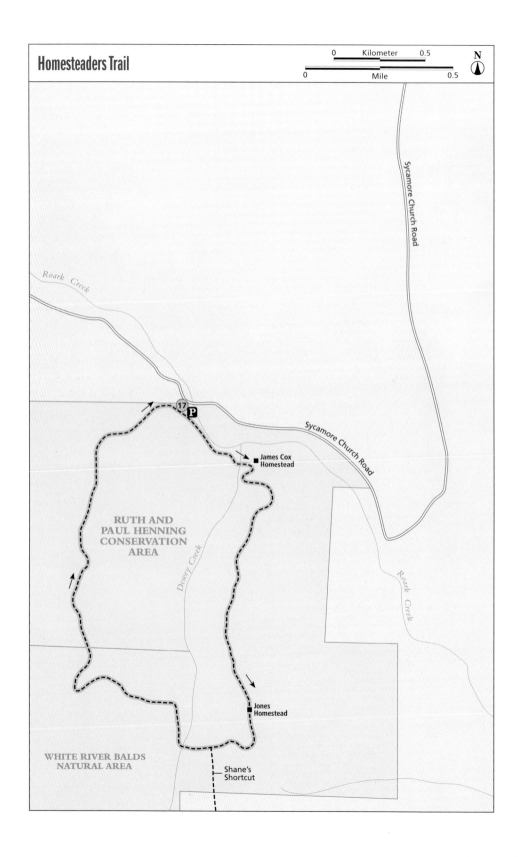

Homesteaders Trail

0   Kilometer   0.5
0   Mile   0.5

N

Sycamore Church Road

Roark Creek

17 P

Sycamore Church Road

■ James Cox
Homestead

RUTH AND
PAUL HENNING
CONSERVATION
AREA

Dewey Creek

Roark Creek

■ Jones
Homestead

WHITE RIVER BALDS
NATURAL AREA

Shane's
Shortcut

This hike focuses on the north side of the conservation area and, as the name suggests, leads visitors past several old homesteads. Be sure to visit the southern side of the conservation area—several short trails there explore the glades.

The trailhead is located on the west side of Roark Creek. From the parking area, cross the low-water bridge and locate the trailhead just south of the road. Turn left (southeast) and follow the orange-blazed trail as it meanders along the bank of Roark Creek. At 0.3 mile, just after crossing Dewey Creek, come to a short spur trail that leads to the James Cox Homestead. The homestead dates back to the mid-1800s, and visitors can see what remains of an old fence and a hand-dug well here. Return to the main trail and continue hiking south.

Come to the Jones Homestead at 1.3 miles. This homestead also dates back to the 1800s. Continue south, passing several more homesteads as the trail begins to turn to the west. Cross Dewey Creek at 1.8 miles and continue west, very shortly reaching the intersection with Shane's Shortcut. This trail connects with the Streamside Trail and the Glade Trail, which explore the southern end of the conservation area. Continue northwest, passing a small but scenic waterfall at 2.1 miles.

From spring through early fall, hikers will likely see an array of wildflowers as they pass through the open glade at 2.3 miles. Look for the white-and-yellow blooms of Queen Anne's lace, Missouri coneflower, and rattlesnake master. From here the trail bends to the north, passing the remains of several more homesteads before returning to the trailhead at 3.6 miles.

Miles and Directions

0.0 Start at the trailhead and follow the orange-blazed trail southeast along the banks of Roark Creek.

0.3 After crossing Dewey Creek reach the spur trail to the James Cox Homestead. Continue south.

1.3 Come to the Jones Homestead. Continue south.

1.8 Cross Dewey Creek and reach the intersection with Shane's Shortcut. Continue northwest.

2.1 Come to a small waterfall and continue northwest.

2.3 Pass through a glade as the trail bends to the north.

3.6 Arrive back at the trailhead.

18 Roaring River State Park: Fire Tower Trail

This half-day loop hike traverses the Roaring River Hills Wild Area and the Roaring River Cove Hardwood Natural Area, both of which provide habitat for several species of plants and animals that are found only in this region of the state. Don't forget your fishing pole for a little pre- or post-hike casting!

Start: From the nature center in Roaring River State Park
Distance: 4.3-mile loop
Hiking time: About 3 hours
Difficulty: Moderate due to modest climbs
Trail surface: Forested trail
Best season: Any
Other trail users: Hikers only
Canine compatibility: Leashed dogs permitted

Fees and permits: None
Schedule: Open year-round
Maps: USGS Eagle Rock; trail map available at park office, nature center, and online
Trail contacts: Roaring River State Park, 12716 Farm Road 2239, Cassville, MO 65625; (417) 8472539; http://mostateparks .com/park/roaring-river-state-park

Finding the trailhead: From Cassville, Missouri, drive 6 miles on MO 112 to the park entrance and continue on MO 112 for 0.9 mile before turning left (east) onto State Highway F. Follow State Highway F for 0.3 mile to Campground #3 and turn right (south) into the area. Then make an immediate left into the nature center parking lot. GPS: N36 34.766' / W93 49.828'

The Hike

One of Missouri's oldest state parks, Roaring River State Park offers a wide variety of recreational activities. Perhaps best known for the trophy trout that swim the waters of Roaring River Spring, the park also offers excellent opportunities for hiking, camping, swimming, and just enjoying the natural beauty of the area.

The park is characterized by the type of terrain one would expect to find in the White River section of the Ozarks. Narrow valleys, deep-blue springs, mountain-like topography, and interesting rock formations make this 4,000-acre park the perfect day-hiking destination. White-tailed deer, striped skunks, minks, and gray foxes are common here. The park is also home to several species that are rare or endangered in Missouri, including the Oklahoma salamander, eastern collared lizard, black bear, and long-tailed weasel.

The Fire Tower Trail traverses the Roaring River Hills Wild Area, which provides ideal habitat for many of the park's rare and endangered plants and animals. It also gives hikers an opportunity to view the southwestern border of the Roaring River Cove Hardwood Natural Area, which contains one of the few old-growth oak-hickory forests in the state.

Locate the trail on the south side of the nature center and begin hiking east and then north on the rocky path. Look for the brown blazes that mark the trail as you

Fire Tower Trail

walk beside MO 112 for about 100 feet. Come to a gravel parking area on the north side of the road, which is signed for the Fire Tower Trail. Follow the obvious rocky path north as it begins a 0.5-mile ascent of a moderately steep ridge through a hardwood forest.

At 0.9 mile reach an intersection with the Deer Leap Trail. Stay right (northeast) and continue along the ridgeline on the Fire Tower Trail. Look for the rare Ozark chinquapin tree as you walk along the ridge. You will reach the old lookout tower at 1.7 miles. Constructed by the Civilian Conservation Corps in the 1930s, the tower provides a good vantage point to take in the tree canopy of the Roaring River Hills Wild Area and Roaring River Cove Hardwood Natural Area. Continue hiking southeast along the ridge.

At 2.2 miles the trail begins to descend the rocky ridge. Come to a glade at 2.8 miles; take a moment to note the contrast between this area and the forest you just hiked through as the trail begins to head southwest.

Fire Tower Trail

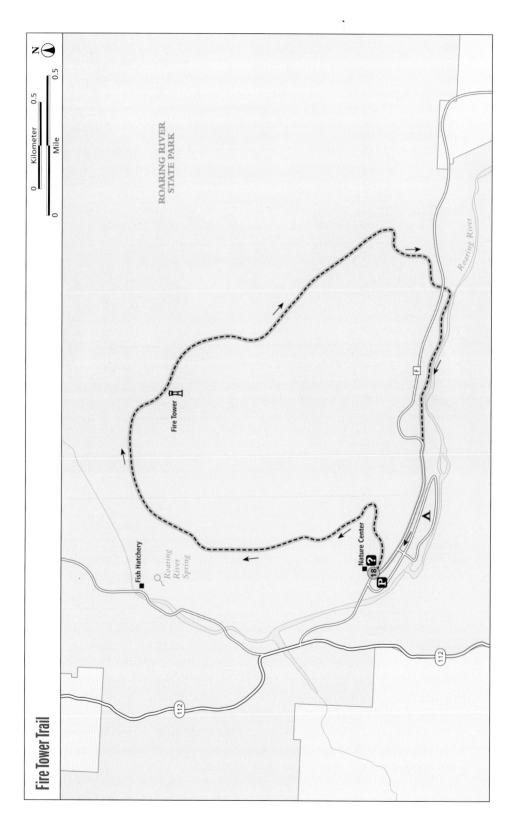

ROARING RIVER STATE PARK

Roaring River

Fire Tower

Fish Hatchery

Roaring River Spring

Nature Center

F

112

112

N

Kilometer
0   0.5

Mile
0   0.5

F

At 3.2 miles the trail turns to the south toward MO 112 and leads to large gravel parking area. Cross MO 112 and find the path heading west on the south side of the road. The trail descends a small hill, crosses a gravel road, and eventually reaches the bank of the Roaring River at 3.4 miles. Continue hiking west until you come to a gate and small parking area at 3.8 miles. Follow the paved park road northwest, past Camp Smokey. Continue northwest on the road until you return to the nature center at 4.3 miles.

Miles and Directions

0.0 Start at the nature center and begin hiking east, then north. Cross MO 112 and come to the gravel parking area on the north side of the road. Follow the trail north.

0.5 Reach the top of the ridge.

0.9 At the intersection with the Deer Leap Trail, stay right (northeast).

1.7 Reach the lookout tower and continue southeast.

2.2 Begin to descend the ridge.

2.8 Come to a glade.

3.2 Cross MO 112 and turn right (west) onto the trail.

3.4 Reach the Roaring River and continue west.

3.8 Come to a gate and parking area and continue northwest on the park road.

4.3 Arrive back at the nature center.

Honorable Mentions

A Chubb Trail

This 14.0-mile out-and-back trail is located in west St. Louis County and begins at Lone Elk County Park. It traverses through Castlewood State Park, where it parallels the Meramec River, coming to an end at West Tyson County Park. It is a popular trail for hiking, mountain biking, and horseback riding but rarely feels crowded. Rugged and hilly at each end, the trail crosses through both dense woodlands and restored prairies, making it an excellent longer option for hiking just a few short miles from St. Louis. From St. Louis, take I-44 West for 17 miles to MO 141 (exit 272). Merge onto North Highway Drive, take a slight right onto MO 141, and then take the ramp to the North Outer Road. Turn left onto Meramec Street and stay straight onto West Outer Road for 2 miles. Turn right onto Lone Elk Park Road. The Chubb Trail is located just before entering through the gates at Lone Elk Park. For more information on the Chubb Trail, contact either St. Louis County Parks at (314) 615-4386 (www.stlouisco.com/parksandrecreation) or Castlewood State Park at (636) 227-4433 (www.mostateparks.com/park/castlewood-state-park).

B Mooner's Hollow Trail

Located in St. Francois State Park, the Mooner's Hollow Trail is a 3.0-mile loop hike. Named for the moonshining activities that once took place in the hollow, the trail travels along Coonville Creek and then up along a rugged ridgeline. Hikers will pass through several glades that offer some brief scenic views and plenty of wildflowers. From Festus, take US 67 South for 19.3 miles before turning left onto Park Road. Drive 0.4 mile on Park Road to the parking area and trailhead on the left. For more information, contact St. Francois State Park, 8920 US 67 N., Bonne Terre, MO 63628; (573) 358-2173; www.mostateparks.com/park/st-francois-state-park.

C Devil's Honeycomb Trail

Located near Potosi, Missouri, Hughes Mountain Natural Area features a combination of glades, hardwood forests, and unique geologic features. Hugh Mountain is considered to be one of the state's geologic wonders. The Devil's Honeycomb Trail traverses the rock outcrops that make up the "honeycomb" design on Hughes Mountain and allows for great views of the surrounding forests and farmland. The rock formations here are thought to be approximately 1.5 billion years old and are some of the oldest exposed rocks in the United States. From Potosi, travel south 11 miles on SH 21, then turn left (east) on Highway M. Continue 8 miles on Highway M until you reach the Missouri Department of Conservation Hughes Mountain Natural Area parking area on the left. For more information, contact the Missouri Department of Conservation at (636) 441-4554 or visit their website at mdc.mo.gov.

D Fire Tower Trail to Long Creek

Located in the Ava District of the Mark Twain National Forest, the 12,413-acre Hercules Glades Wilderness Area has over 40 miles of trails. The trails here are as rugged as the landscape and not well marked. While the Lookout Tower Trail to Long Creek is fairly straightforward, any exploration beyond this point will require a map, compass, and topographical map. Narrow hollows, open glades, and steep, rocky hillsides characterize the area, making it one of the state's finest destinations for those seeking a true wilderness experience. From Springfield, drive south on US 65 for 5.8 miles to US 60. Turn left (east) onto US 60 and drive 6.6 miles to MO 125. Turn right (south) onto MO 125 and continue for 33.3 miles until you reach MO 125/MO 76. Turn left (east), staying on MO 125/MO 76 for 0.7 mile and then turn right (south) onto MO 125. Drive 7 miles on MO 125 to the Hercules Glades Wilderness and turn to the right (west). Drive 0.1 mile to the parking area. For more information, contact the US Forest Service, Mark Twain National Forest, Ava/Cassville/Willow Springs Ranger District, 1103 S. Jefferson, Ava, MO 65608; (417) 683-4428; fs.usda.gov.

E Lakeside Forest Wilderness Area Trails 1 and 2

Located within the Branson city limits, the 130-acre Lakeside Forest Wilderness Area sits above the well-known waters of Lake Taneycomo. The area is managed by the Branson Parks and Recreation Department and has been set aside to preserve and protect a portion of the natural beauty found here in the Ozarks. There are two separate trails here that allow visitors to explore this unique park. Both boast beautiful natural scenery and each makes a fine day hike. We suggest combining the two trails to form a 3.0-mile hike through lush woodlands, along steep bluffs, and across rocky glades. A picnic area, restrooms, and water are located near the large, gravel parking area. From the MO 76/Main Street exit on US 65 in Branson, turn right (west) onto MO 76/Main Street and drive 1.1 miles to Fall Creek Road. Turn left (south) onto Fall Creek Road and then make a quick left into the Lakeside Forest Wilderness Area parking lot. For more information, contact the Branson Parks and Recreation Department, 1500 Branson Hills Pkwy., Branson, MO 65716; (417) 335-2368; bransonparksandrecreation.com.

Arkansas Region

The rugged beauty of the Arkansas Ozark region provides visitors with a thrilling arrangement of year-round hiking opportunities. The nineteen hikes featured in this section explore a diversity of terrains that include spectacular views, shimmering mountain rivers, clear-water lakes, impressive waterfalls, and curiosity-provoking caves and caverns. Quaint mountain towns provide a glimpse into Arkansas's rich history and an opportunity to experience the best of the region's culture.

Stretching across the northern part of Arkansas, the Ozarks span from the western border to the north-central portion of the state. Arkansans generally refer to this area as the Arkansas Ozark Mountain Region. The area offers several "destination" recreational areas: the Buffalo River, Bull Shoals, Norfork Lake, and the White River. All of these areas' focus seems to be on fishing, but trust us, there is much more to the area than fish. The Buffalo National River is the setting for many adventures in the Ozarks. America's first designated National River, the Buffalo National River flows, undammed, for over 135 miles. The river itself is a destination for countless paddlers each year, but the surrounding landscape makes it an ideal location for nature lovers and hikers. In the north-central and eastern parts of the Arkansas Ozarks are Bull Shoals Lake and Norfork Lake. The largest lake in Arkansas, Bull Shoals Lake is known for the record-size bass that are pulled from its waters, but it also offers several good opportunities for hiking. Norfork Lake is also a popular destination with sportsmen/women, as well as swimmers, beachgoers, hikers, and other outdoor enthusiasts. Beginning near Fayetteville, the White River flows through both the Missouri and Arkansas Ozarks. The first of eight dams on the White River is the Powersite Dam in Branson, Missouri, which forms Lake Taneycomo.

In addition to these areas, Arkansas is home to a fabulous state park system. Many of the hikes in the Arkansas Ozarks are located on land managed by Arkansas State Parks. You can expect well-groomed trails, interpretive hikes and events, good camping, beautiful visitor centers, and even swimming pools at many of these state parks, making them real options for vacation destinations.

19 Devil's Den State Park: Yellow Rock Trail

Hike the Yellow Rock Trail in the fall for the best views that it can offer during prime fall foliage season. Don't be fooled though: This 2.7-mile lollipop hike offers some great views year-round. Hikers who make their way to the Yellow Rock Overlook will not only be rewarded with great views of the park below, they may also catch glimpses of birds of prey that circle the valley in this area.

Start: From the Yellow Rock Trailhead in Devil's Den State Park
Distance: 2.7-mile lollipop
Hiking time: About 2 to 3 hours
Difficulty: Easy
Trail surface: Forested path, dirt trail
Best season: Best in spring from Mar through May and fall from Sept to Nov for the fall foliage
Other trail users: Hikers only

Canine compatibility: Leashed dogs permitted
Fees and permits: None
Schedule: Park is open year-round
Maps: USGS Strickler; trail maps are available at the park's visitor center
Trail contacts: Devil's Den State Park, 11333 W. Arkansas Hwy. 74, West Fork, AR 72774; (479) 761-3325; www.arkansasstateparks .com/devilsden

Finding the trailhead: From West Fork, Arkansas, take I-540 south for about 7 miles to exit 45, then turn right (west) onto AR 74. Drive 3.5 miles on AR 74 to the park entrance and continue driving. At 7.1 miles from I-540, turn right onto the unnamed park road just after crossing Lee Creek. A sign here directs visitors to Camp Area A. At 7.2 miles park on the right (south) side of the road, then walk a short distance back west to the Yellow Rock Trailhead on the north side of the road. GPS: N35 46.930' / W94 14.810'

The Hike

Surrounded by the Ozark National Forest, Devil's Den State Park is considered an Arkansas icon by locals as well as by many out-of-state visitors. The park, located in the Boston Mountains, is neatly tucked away in the Lee Creek Valley and is a result of the hard work of the Civilian Conservation Corps (CCC) and Franklin D. Roosevelt's New Deal. The CCC built the park back in the 1930s and did a wonderful job blending the rustic-style CCC buildings and structures with the surrounding natural beauty of the Ozarks. Structures built by the CCC include several stone buildings, a native stone dam that has created Lake Devil, a restaurant, numerous stone walls, bridges, trails, and the Yellow Rock Overlook, which can be accessed by vehicle off of AR 170 or via the Yellow Rock Trail. All the efforts by the CCC have not gone unnoticed as Devil's Den State Park has been designated a National Historic District.

Locate the Yellow Rock Trailhead on the north side of the unnamed park road and just west of the trailhead parking area and begin hiking north. The trail follows along a rocky trail that is very pleasant, gradually ascends, and passes through a

lush oak-hickory forest. Continue for 0.5 mile up the trail as it passes along several beautiful rocky bluffs until you arrive at a trail junction. This junction is the beginning of the loop portion of the hike and is also the level area above the bluff known as a bench. Benches are horizontal layers of rock that are common formations on plateaus like the one found in the Ozarks. Stay left (west) here to continue hiking the loop portion in a clockwise manner. The trail levels out here, and you will travel through a beautiful hardwood forest that is full of amazing wildflowers and dogwood trees in the spring and wonderful fall foliage in autumn. At 1.0 mile you will come to a second fork in the trail. Turn right (north) to continue hiking on the Yellow Rock Trail toward Yellow Rock. Turning left (southwest) here takes you over a small footbridge and then a climb up to the Yellow Rock Overlook, which is just off of AR 170.

View from Yellow Rock Trail

Continuing toward Yellow Rock, you will hike through the forest along the dirt path, and the trail eventually becomes more rocky and rugged as you get closer to the Yellow Rock bluff. Just after beginning a descent, you will arrive at Yellow Rock at 1.8 miles. Yellow Rock earned its name because of the yellow iron oxide stains that have covered the bluff face. Spend a little time here to soak up the views and enjoy watching the birds of prey circle. Reenter the forest from the overlook area and continue down the trail as it gradually descends near the bluff ledge. Come to the end of the loop portion of the hike at 2.2 miles and stay left (south) to return to the trailhead and parking area. Reach the trailhead at 2.7 miles.

◀ *Rocky bluff along Yellow Rock Trail*

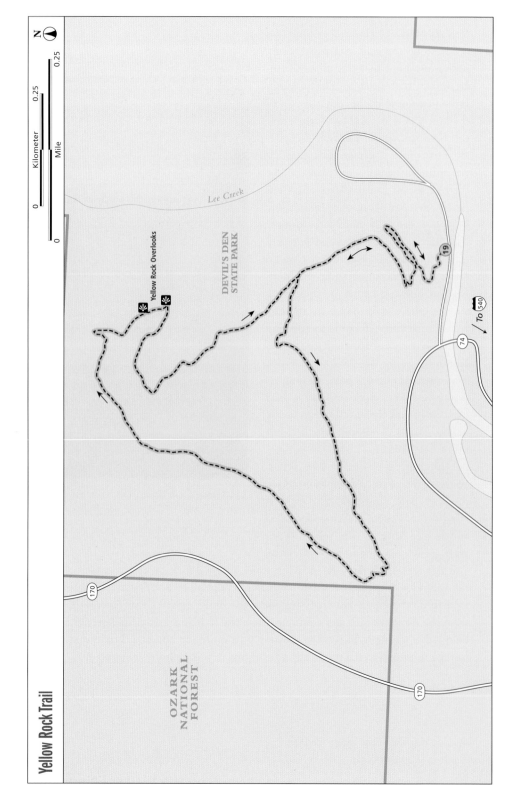

Yellow Rock Trail

Yellow Rock Overlooks

DEVIL'S DEN STATE PARK

Lee Creek

OZARK NATIONAL FOREST

170

170

74

19

To 540

Kilometer

Mile

0   0.25

0   0.25

N

Miles and Directions

0.0 Locate the Yellow Rock Trailhead on the north side of the unnamed park road just west of the parking area and begin hiking north. After just a few feet, pass an information kiosk and trail register before the trail becomes rocky and begins a gradual ascent.

0.5 Reach a fork in the trail. Stay left (west) to begin the loop portion of this hike. Right (north) will be your return trail.

1.0 Turn right (north) to continue on the loop and head toward Yellow Rock. Left (southwest) leads to an overlook off of AR 170.

1.8 Arrive at Yellow Rock and the overlook of the valley.

2.2 The loop portion of the hike ends. Stay left (south) to return to the trailhead and parking area.

2.7 Arrive back at the trailhead and parking area.

20 Devil's Den State Park: Devil's Den Trail

Highlights of this hike include several natural geological features that were left behind in an area once believed to have been a shallow ocean. Devil's Den Cave, the Devil's Icebox, a cold spring, and a beautiful set of waterfalls all highlight this self-guided trail. Views and access to Lee Creek are also included in this hike, making it an ideal hike for those hot summer days when you are looking for places to cool off. Did we mention the cool breezes that continually blow out of the caves?

Start: From the visitor center in Devil's Den State Park
Distance: 1.5-mile lollipop
Hiking time: About 2 hours
Difficulty: Easy
Trail surface: Forested path, dirt trail, road crossings
Best season: Best in spring from Mar through May and fall from Sept to Nov for the fall foliage

Other trail users: Hikers only
Canine compatibility: Leashed dogs permitted
Fees and permits: None
Schedule: Park is open year-round
Maps: USGS Strickler; trail maps are available at the park's visitor center
Trail contacts: Devil's Den State Park, 11333 W. Arkansas Hwy. 74, West Fork, AR 72774; (479) 761-3325; www.arkansasstateparks .com/devilsden

Finding the trailhead: From West Fork, Arkansas, take I-540 south for about 7 miles to exit 45, then turn right (west) onto AR 74. Drive 3.5 miles on AR 74 to the park entrance and continue driving. At 7 miles from I-540, turn left into the visitor center parking area and locate the trail at the southeast corner of the building. GPS: N35 46.789' / W94 15.010'

The Hike

The Devil's Den Trail in Devil's Den State Park is another one of those geologic wonders that received a "Devil" name from those who found it. Don't let the name fool you, as this park and trail will remind you of nothing like a devil. The park is rich with history, beauty, and recreational opportunities. Visitors can embark on a scenic driving tour that visits old homestead sites and travels through the beautiful Boston Mountains, ride for miles and miles on the well-developed equestrian trails, camp in one of the numerous campsites along the valley floor and along Lee Creek, and can of course hike along some of the most beautiful trails in the Ozarks. The scenic Devil's Den Trail has actually found itself on the National Recreation Trails System list that is created by the Department of Interior and the National Park Service. A trail needs to be well developed and

Waterfall on Devil's Den Trail ▷

accessible to the public, and must possess a significant cultural or natural quality to qualify for the National Recreation Trail System listing.

Locate the trailhead at the southeast corner of the Devil's Den State Park visitor center. Parking is available here and in a few other surrounding places that offer access to the trail. We recommend starting here so you can stop into the visitor center first and pick up a self-guiding brochure for the trail. After picking up the brochure, begin hiking north behind the visitor center. Cross AR 74 and come to the first of two forks in the trail at 0.1 mile. Stay right (east) to continue on the main trail. Left (northwest) leads you to one of the additional parking areas for this trail. Continue hiking through the large oak and hickory forest to 0.2 mile and the second fork in the trail. Turn right (south) to begin the loop portion of the hike. Left (north) will be your return trail.

Hike south as the amazing geology of the area becomes more and more apparent. The trail makes a sharp turn east and you will soon approach the Devil's Den Cave. The cave extends about 550 feet into the mountainside. Many people believe that the cave was an old hideout for outlaws that frequented the area. Today it is home to numerous bats that are endangered by white-nose syndrome, a fungal disease that has caused massive destruction to the bat populations. Some species of bats have seen as much as a 95 percent mortality rate according to the US Fish and Wildlife Service. Please respect the land manager's requests to stay out of caves in an effort to protect these bats from further harm.

After enjoying the cave continue hiking northeast along the trail as it climbs up and down the rocky and rugged area. At 0.6 mile you will come to the Devil's Icebox. These large crevices were believed to have formed from a major slide just south of the area. The temperatures of the caves and crevices in the area average around 55°F to 60°F year-round. However, the unusual airflow that has been created at the Devil's Icebox makes the air feel even cooler, making this an ideal place for hikers to cool off. Continuing northeast on the trail, you will reach the Twin Falls waterfall at 0.9 mile. This beautiful set of falls has two cascades during wet weather. The trail will take hikers directly under the falls. Be prepared to get wet if the area has been getting a good amount of rain when you visit.

After leaving the falls the trail direction changes to west and then southwest and begins descending down from the rocky areas of the hillside. At 1.0 mile the area becomes very lush and you will pass by the Cold Springs, which are running off into Lee Creek to your right (west). The trail continues along Lee Creek for the next section and reaches the end of the loop portion of the hike at 1.3 miles. Turn right (west) to return to the trailhead and visitor center parking area. Arrive back at the trailhead and parking area at 1.5 miles.

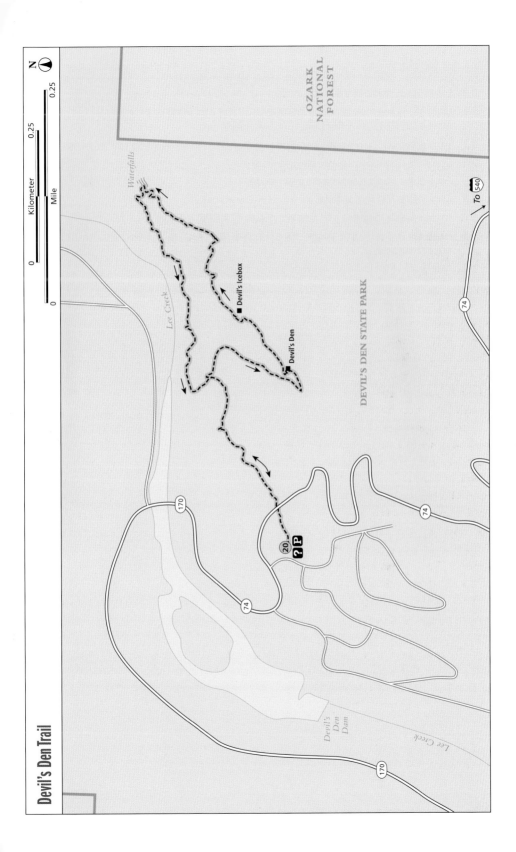

Devil's Den Trail

OZARK
NATIONAL
FOREST

DEVIL'S DEN STATE PARK

Waterfalls

Lee Creek

Devil's Icebox

Devil's Den

Devil's
Den
Dam

Lee Creek

To 540

N

Kilometer
0   0.25   0.25
Mile

Miles and Directions

0.0 Locate the trailhead at the southeast corner of the visitor center and begin hiking north.

0.1 Cross AR 74 and then come to a fork in the trail. Stay right (east) on the main trail. Left (northwest) leads to another Devil's Den Trail parking area.

0.2 Turn right (south) to begin the loop portion of the hike. Left (north) will be your return trail.

0.4 Reach the Devil's Den Cave on the right (south).

0.6 Arrive at the Devil's Icebox on the right (south).

0.9 Come to the Twin Falls waterfall.

1.0 The trail travels through a lush area and passes by the Cold Springs.

1.3 Reach the end of the loop portion of the hike. Turn right (west) to return to the trailhead and parking area.

1.5 Arrive back at the trailhead and visitor center parking area.

21 Ozark Highlands Trail: Lake Fort Smith State Park to Frog Bayou

Discover the Ozarks on the still-developing Ozark Highlands Trail. This hike begins at the western terminus of the trail at Lake Fort Smith State Park. The trail follows along a beautiful section of Lake Fort Smith and offers hikers several opportunities to enjoy the beauty of the state park, the Ozark Highlands Trail, and the surrounding Ozarks. Hikers looking for an extended trip only need to continue hiking past the turnaround that is described in this guide.

Start: From the Ozark Highlands Trailhead in Lake Fort Smith State Park

Distance: 5.4 miles out and back

Hiking time: About 3 to 4 hours

Difficulty: Moderate due to length

Trail surface: Forested path, paved trail, dirt path

Best season: Best in spring from Mar through May and fall from Sept to Nov for the fall foliage

Other trail users: Hikers only

Canine compatibility: Leashed dogs permitted

Fees and permits: None

Schedule: Open year-round

Maps: USGS Mountainburg; trail map available at the Lake Fort Smith State Park Visitor Center; Ozark Highlands Trail Guide available at www.timernst.com/Products/OHT.html

Trail contacts: Lake Fort Smith State Park, PO Box 4, Mountainburg, AR 72946; (479) 369-2469; www.arkansasstateparks.com/lakefortsmith. Ozark Highlands Trail Association, PO Box 4065, Fayetteville, AR 72702-4065; ozarkhighlandstrail.com

Finding the trailhead: From Mountainburg, Arkansas, drive northeast on AR 282 East/US 71 North for 6.7 miles. Turn right (east) onto AR 400/Shepherd Springs Road and drive 2 miles to the Lake Fort Smith State Park visitor center and trailhead parking area on the right (south). GPS: N35 41.730' / W94 07.100'

The Hike

The Ozark Highlands Trail is a work of art that is still in progress. The trail is considered by many as one of the most scenic trails in the United States. The trail begins at Lake Fort Smith State Park, traverses the highlands of the Ozarks, and currently ends at US 65 near the Tyler Bend Recreation Area, around 253 miles total. Hikers traveling along this trail will have the opportunity to see beautiful vistas, cover mountainous terrain, cross numerous creeks and streams, see hundreds of waterfalls, and encounter unique rock outcroppings. Access-wise, the trail crosses more than fifty forest roads and highways and passes through almost twenty designated campgrounds. All these access points allow for numerous day-hiking and backpacking options. Please sign in at trailhead registers for emergency purposes and to help the Ozark Highlands Trail Association track trail usage.

Frog Bayou on Ozark Highland Trail

The western terminus of the trail is located in Lake Fort Smith State Park. The park was designated a state park in 1973 after serving as a city park for about forty years before that. The park was closed for a short period of time while the reservoir was enlarged to properly service the growing city of Fort Smith. The park reopened in its current location in 2008. The new park offers camping, cabin lodging, picnic sites, a marina, a swimming pool, and several other facilities that make Lake Fort Smith State Park a great getaway destination. In addition to all the facilities that the park offers, it is also a gateway to outdoor adventures in the Boston Mountains, including the Ozark Highlands Trail.

On the east side of the Lake Fort Smith State Park visitor center you will locate the Ozark Highlands Trailhead sign. Begin hiking south around the side of the visitor center on the paved sidewalk. Follow the sidewalk as it winds around behind the visitor center and the sidewalk ends and the trail becomes a dirt path at 0.1 mile. Hike east along the trail as it travels between the campground to the north and the lake to the south. This section of the Ozark Highlands Trail travels along Lake Fort Smith

Ozark Highlands Trail: Lake Fort Smith State Park to Frog Bayou

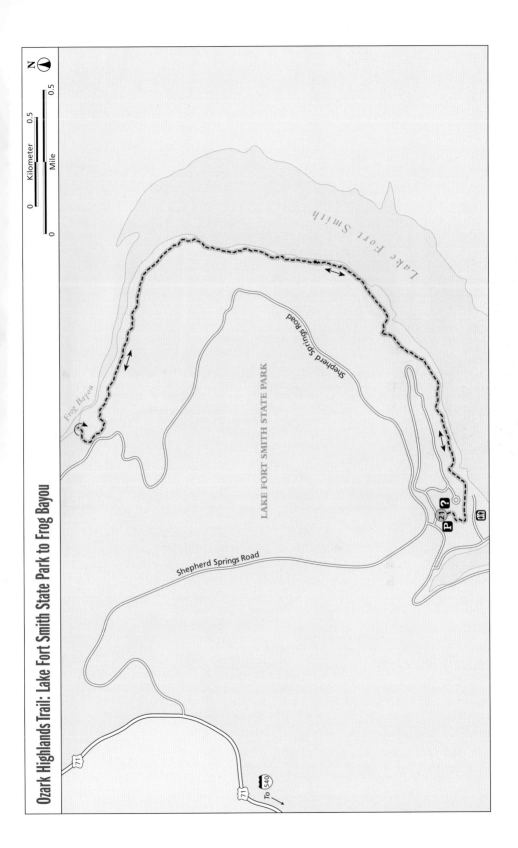

the entire way to Frog Bayou. While doing so, hikers should expect to cross several creeks and streams that run into the lake. During periods of precipitation you may get your feet wet.

At 0.8 mile a trail comes in from the left (north). This trail leads to the campground. Stay right (east) to continue hiking on the Ozark Highlands Trail. Not long after this trail junction, the trail can become a little tough to navigate during the summer months when the path becomes overgrown. Watch for the white blazes on the trees to keep you on track. You'll reach a set of twelve man-made wooden stairs at 1.4 miles that will let you know you are still headed in the right direction. Continue hiking as the trail begins to head in a northeast direction. At 2.5 miles you cross a larger inlet and then the trail makes a sharp left (north) up a hill. Watch for the white blazes here again as you could accidently follow a service road that leads to the right (east).

Eventually the trail drops down to the lake and comes to Frog Bayou at 2.7 miles. If you plan to hike past this point you should be prepared to get your feet wet as the Frog Bayou crossing can be wide and deep. Turn around here if you are not continuing and follow the trail back to the Lake Fort Smith State Park Visitor Center and parking area at 5.4 miles.

Miles and Directions

0.0 Locate the Ozark Highlands Trailhead sign on the east side of the Lake Fort Smith State Park Visitor Center and begin hiking south on the paved trail.

0.1 The sidewalk ends behind the visitor center and becomes a dirt path.

0.8 Come to a trail that connects to the Ozark Highlands Trail from the left (north). Stay right (east) to continue on the Ozark Highlands Trail. The trail to the left leads to a campground.

1.4 Reach a set of twelve man-made wooden stairs.

2.5 Just after an inlet crossing, the trail makes a sharp left (north) up a hill. Look for the white blazes.

2.7 Arrive at Frog Bayou.

5.4 Arrive back at the Ozark Highlands Trailhead and the Lake Fort Smith State Park Visitor Center.

◁ *Ozark Highland Trail*

22 White Rock Mountain Recreation Area: Rim Trail

The White Rock Mountain Recreation Area is one of the highest points along the Ozark Highlands Trail and provides beautiful views of the surrounding mountains in all directions. The Rim Trail and the stone-wall overlook buildings that have been built around the rim of the mountain make for an ideal hike. Don't forget your camera for this hike as the views can be quite stunning, especially in the fall.

Start: From the trailhead at White Rock Mountain Recreation Area
Distance: 2.2-mile loop
Hiking time: About 1 to 2 hours
Difficulty: Easy due to flat terrain
Trail surface: Forested trail, dirt path, gravel road crossing
Best season: Best in spring from Mar through May for the wildflower displays and fall from Sept to Nov for the fall foliage

Other trail users: Hikers only
Canine compatibility: Leashed dogs permitted
Fees and permits: None
Schedule: Open year-round
Maps: USGS Bidville; Forest Service map can be printed out at www.fs.usda.gov/main/osfnf/maps-pubs
Trail contacts: Forest Service, 605 W. Main St., Russellville, AR 72801; (479) 964-7200; www.fs.usda.gov

Finding the trailhead: From Mulberry, Arkansas, take AR 215 north for 15 miles, then turn left (west) to follow Bliss Ridge Road toward Shores Lake and White Rock Mountain. At 23 miles turn left (west) onto FR 1003/1505/White Rock Mountain Road and drive to 25.3 miles. Turn right toward White Rock Mountain onto FR 1505/Hurricane Road. Drive to 25.8 miles and turn right again toward White Rock Mountain Recreation Area. Arrive at the parking area and trailhead at 26.7 miles. GPS: N35 41.360' / W93 57.280'

The Hike

Visiting White Rock Mountain Recreation Area in the Ozark National Forest promises to be a treat for most if not all visitors. Prepare to step into the past when you see the three natural stone cabins and the old lodge on White Rock Mountain that was built by the Civilian Conservation Corps in the 1930s. Over the years wind, rain, and other elements caused natural deterioration of the buildings and prompted a volunteer group to begin a project to renovate the structures in 1987. The cabins and lodge were restored in 1991 through those efforts, and the cabins are still available to rent today.

White Rock Mountain is 2,260 feet above sea level and received its name from the appearance of the lichen on the bluffs that cause them to look white from a distance. These white and very high bluffs surround the area, and the Rim Trail travels along the bluffs almost the entire way. The White Rock Mountain Recreation Area serves as the hub for a few different trail systems. In addition to the 2.2-mile loop trail described here, hikers can access the Ozark Highlands Trail as well as a 13.4-mile loop

View from Rim Trail

trail to Shores Lake. And did we mention that the recreation area offers some of the best views of the surrounding Ozark Mountains?

Drive past the camping area, the day-use area, and the stone cabins and park at the trailhead at the southeast part of the recreation area. From the trailhead, begin hiking east along the gravel road. Just past the last stone cabin, the gravel road ends and the dirt packed trail begins. Continue hiking on the trail to 0.1 mile, where you will come to a trail junction. Turn left (east) onto the Rim Trail. Heading straight (southeast) leads to the Ozark Highlands Trail and the Shores Lake Loop, and right (west) will be your return trail. The Rim Trail does just as its name suggests: It travels around the rim of White Rock Mountain. The trail is well maintained but comes very close to several steep drop-offs along the way. Be very cautious while hiking, watch your footing, and keep a close eye on children if you bring them with you.

At 0.9 mile you will come to the first of four shelters that have been built along the trail. The shelters are beautifully constructed from stone and offer an excellent place to sit and take in the views all around. From the North Shelter, continue hiking north as the trail eventually turns west and then crosses the gravel FR 1535 at 1.1 miles. After crossing the road the trail turns south, and you will soon reach the West Shelter at 1.4 miles. At 1.8 miles arrive at the Sunset Shelter and picnic area. This shelter is a great spot to enjoy a longer break or lunch or obviously a good sunset in the evening. From the Sunset Shelter the trail heads east along the southern rim of

Rim Trail

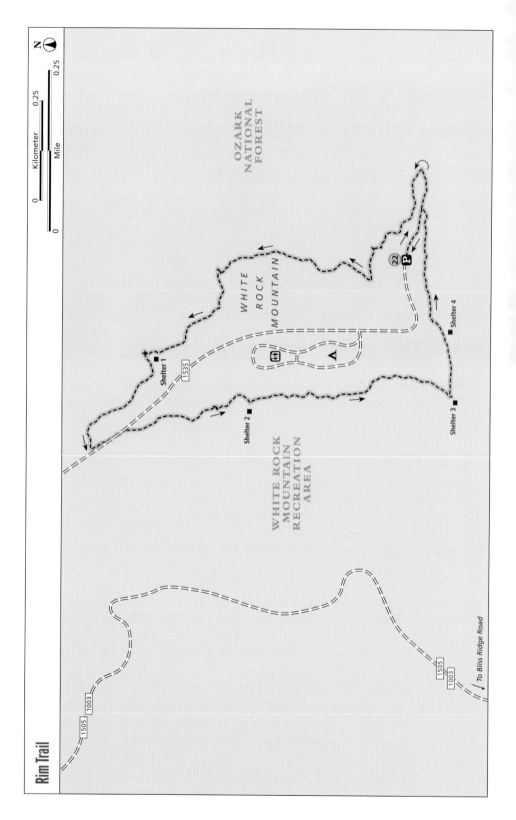

N

| Kilometer | 0 | 0.25 |
| Mile | 0 | 0.25 |

OZARK
NATIONAL
FOREST

WHITE ROCK
MOUNTAIN

WHITE ROCK
MOUNTAIN
RECREATION
AREA

1535

Shelter 1

Shelter 2

Shelter 3

Shelter 4

22

P

1505 1003

1505
1003

To Bliss Ridge Road

Shelter on Rim Trail

the mountain and quickly approaches the final shelter on the trail at 1.9 miles. Leave the South Shelter continuing east, where you will hike past the stone cabins to the north and then reach the end of the Rim Trail at 2.1 miles. Turn left (northwest) to return to the trailhead and parking area at 2.2 miles.

Miles and Directions

0.0 Head east from the parking area and trailhead.

0.1 Come to a trail junction. Turn left (east) to stay on the Rim Trail. Heading straight (southeast) leads to the Ozark Highlands Trail. Right (west) is your return trail.

0.9 Arrive at the first of four hiker shelters, North Shelter.

1.1 Cross the gravel FR 1535.

1.4 Come to the second of four hiker shelters, West Shelter.

1.8 Arrive at the third of four shelters, Sunset Shelter, and a large picnic area. A trail to the left (northeast) leads to a day-use parking area. Continue east on the Rim Trail.

1.9 Come to the final shelter, South Shelter.

2.1 Reach the end of the Rim Trail and turn left (northwest) to return to the parking area and trailhead.

2.2 Arrive back at the parking area and trailhead.

23 Hobbs State Park: Pigeon Roost Trail

This day hike or beginner-level overnight backpacking trail offers some great views of the northern Arkansas Ozarks. Hobbs State Park, like other Arkansas state parks, does an amazing job maintaining their trails and backcountry campsites. Hikers and backpackers looking for a peaceful getaway on a beautiful trail can't do much better than the Pigeon Roost Trail or other trails found here in Hobbs State Park and Conservation Area. The trail offers five designated backcountry campsites.

Start: From the Pigeon Roost Trailhead and parking lot in Hobbs State Park
Distance: 8.4-mile lollipop
Hiking time: About 5 hours
Difficulty: Moderate due to length and light elevation gains
Trail surface: Dirt path, forested trail
Best season: Early spring and late fall for cooler temperatures and wildflowers
Other trail users: Hikers only

Canine compatibility: Leashed dogs permitted
Fees and permits: None
Schedule: Open year-round
Maps: USGS Forum; trail map available at Hobbs State Park Visitor Center
Trail contacts: Hobbs State Park-Conservation Area, 20201 E. Highway 12, Rogers, AR 72756; (479) 789-5000; www.arkansasstate parks.com/hobbsstateparkconservationarea

Finding the trailhead: From Rogers, Arkansas, drive 13.1 miles on AR 12 past the Hobbs State Park Visitor Center on the right (south) to the Pigeon Roost Trailhead and parking area on the left (north). GPS: N36 17.430' / W93 55.840'

The Hike

Hobbs State Park, Arkansas's largest state park in land area, covers 12,045 acres along the southern shores of 28,370-acre Beaver Lake. In fact, nearly 22 of the park's 60 miles of border stretch along the shores of Beaver Lake. This large piece of Ozark landscape consists of plateaus, ridges, valleys, and streams, and features an upland forest filled with pine, oak, and hickory. There are numerous water features throughout the park, including a disappearing stream and springs that, over time, have helped carve many hollows and caves through the land. The Hobbs State Park–Conservation Area is jointly managed by Arkansas State Parks, the Arkansas Natural Heritage Commission, and the Arkansas Game and Fish Commission. This joint effort continues to provide numerous recreational opportunities to the quickly growing northwest region of Arkansas.

The park offers few yet very impressive facilities. The 17,531-square-foot visitor center was built in 2009 and offers information kiosks, classroom spaces, a retail store,

Pigeon Roost Trail ▷

Van Winkle Hollow

restrooms, and park offices. The park is also home to the only public outdoor shooting range in Arkansas with a bullet trap. Other facilities, like picnic areas and camping areas, are in the planning phases. What the park may lack in man-made facilities it more than makes up for with all the hiking and riding opportunities. Six trails and trail systems are scattered throughout the park and range in length and difficulty from easy quarter-mile historical hikes to the longer 8.4-mile backpacking option that is offered on the Pigeon Roost Trail and the numerous options that are offered on the Hidden Diversity Multi-Use Trail system.

Locate the Pigeon Roost Trail at the northwest corner of the parking area and begin hiking north on the dirt packed and forested trail. The trail begins descending down a ridge through a beautiful oak, hickory, and pine forest. You will come to the beginning of the loop portion of the hike at 0.7 mile. The Pigeon Roost Trail is made up of two loops, the Dry Creek Loop and the Huckleberry Loop. Turn left (west) here to begin hiking on the first loop, the Dry Creek Loop. The trail climbs gradually up in a southwest direction and then turns west. Not long after turning west, you will

Pigeon Roost Trail

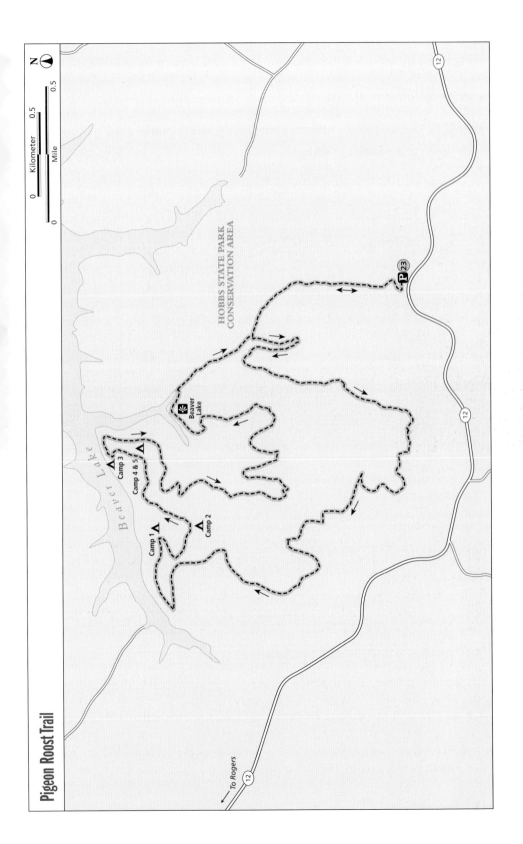

HOBBS STATE PARK
CONSERVATION AREA

Beaver Lake

Beaver Lake

Camp 1

Camp 2

Camp 3

Camp 4 & 5

To Rogers

N

0   Kilometer   0.5

0   Mile   0.5

P 23

12

12

12

encounter a trail junction at 1.9 miles. The Dry Creek Loop turns right (north). For this description, stay left (west) to continue on what is the Huckleberry Loop Trail. Continue hiking west and then northwest as the trail climbs up a ridge and soon comes to a sign at 2.8 miles that indicates CAMPSITES AHEAD. The trail travels along a ridgetop for the next several miles to where hikers who intend to camp will come across a series of campsites. Views of Van Winkle Hollow, an inlet to Beaver Lake, are offered along this section of the trail to the north.

Come to the first of five campsites at 4.0 miles. The second campsite is just a bit farther down the trail at 4.3 miles and Campsites 3, 4, and 5 are just a bit farther at 4.6 miles. All five campsites sit up high on the ridge and have great views and access to Beaver Lake. Once past the campsites, the trail begins to descend slowly down the ridge you have been traveling along. You will come to the end of the Huckleberry Loop Trail at 6.2 miles, where there is another trail junction and the Dry Creek Loop comes up from the right (south). Stay left (northeast) to continue the hike on the Dry Creek Loop. The trail eventually makes its way down to Beaver Lake for good water access and a nice view of the lake at 6.7 miles. At 7.7 miles you'll reach the end of the loop portion of the hike. Turn left (southeast) to return to the Pigeon Roost Trailhead and parking area at 8.4 miles.

Miles and Directions

0.0   Locate the Pigeon Roost Trail at the northwest corner of the parking area and begin hiking north.

0.7   Come to a trail junction and turn left (south) to begin the loop portion of the trail.

1.9   The Dry Creek Loop Trail (option) comes in from the right (north). Stay left (west) to continue on the Huckleberry Loop Trail.

2.8   Reach a CAMPSITES AHEAD sign.

4.0   Come to campsite 1.

4.3   Come to campsite 2.

4.6   Come to campsites 3, 4, and 5.

6.2   The Dry Creek Loop Trail comes in from the right (south). Stay left (northeast) to continue on the main loop trail.

6.7   Arrive at a good Beaver Lake overlook.

7.7   Reach the end of loop portion of the trail. Turn left (southeast) to return to the trailhead and parking area.

8.4   Arrive back at the Pigeon Roost Trailhead and parking area.

24 Hobbs State Park: Bashore Ridge Loop Trail

This 4.3-mile lollipop hike is an easy stroll along Hobbs State Park's multiuse trail. The hike along Bashore Ridge will take hikers to a scenic overlook of Blackburn Creek, a large inlet that connects to the much larger Beaver Lake. Watch for other users along the popular Hidden Diversity Multi-Use Trail system including bikers, horses, and runners. In the spring the park even hosts a 50k race on this trail system. Be sure to check park events in advance in order to plan accordingly.

Start: From the Hidden Diversity Multi-Use Trailhead and parking lot in Hobbs State Park
Distance: 4.3-mile lollipop
Hiking time: About 2 to 2.5 hours
Difficulty: Easy
Trail surface: Dirt path, forested trail
Best season: Early spring and late fall for cooler temperatures
Other trail users: Bikers and equestrians

Canine compatibility: Leashed dogs permitted
Fees and permits: None
Schedule: Open year-round
Maps: USGS Forum; trail map available at Hobbs State Park Visitor Center
Trail contacts: Hobbs State Park-Conservation Area, 20201 East Hwy. 12, Rogers, AR 72756; (479) 789-5000; www.arkansasstateparks .com/hobbsstateparkconservationarea

Finding the trailhead: From Rogers, Arkansas, drive 10.6 miles on AR 12 to Piney Road. Turn right (south) onto Piney Road and continue 10.9 miles to the Hidden Diversity Multi-Use Trailhead and parking area on the right (west). GPS: N36 17.490' / W93 58.630'

The Hike

Hobbs State Park shares several borders with Beaver Lake in northwest Arkansas. The lake has become known by many in the area as the Jewel of the Ozarks. Beaver Lake is a man-made reservoir nestled in the Ozark Highlands that was formed by a dam across the White River. The lake was completed back in 1966 and was the first in a series of three reservoirs on the White River that were all built by the US Army Corps of Engineers. The headwaters of the White River originate in the Boston Mountains in Arkansas, then flow north into Missouri, and then south back into Arkansas.

With almost 500 miles of shoreline and almost 32,000 surface acres, Beaver Lake offers some of the best in recreational opportunities for outdoor enthusiasts in northwest Arkansas. The towering limestone bluffs, crevices, and a diversity of wildlife and birds afford hikers, bikers, boaters, and nature lovers numerous hours of enjoyment throughout the year. The crystal-clear waters of the lake call to boaters, campers, fishermen, and scuba divers alike. Beaver Lake is also the largest supplier of water for northwest Arkansas. The Bashore Ridge Loop Trail is just one of the trails in Hobbs State Park that offers a beautiful viewpoint of Beaver Lake.

Locate the trail on the west side of the Hidden Diversity Multi-Use Trail system trailhead and parking area and begin hiking north on the signed Bashore Ridge Loop/

Trail intersection near Bashore Ridge Loop Trailhead

Dutton Hollow Trails. Be sure to watch for other trail users during this hike. The entire multiuse trail is very popular with bikers. The trail snakes through the forest for the first section of the hike and reaches a trail junction at 0.6 mile. Stay left (southwest) at this junction onto the Bashore Ridge Loop Trail; turning right (west) will take you on the Dutton Hollow Trail. Just a short distance after turning onto the Bashore Ridge Loop Trail, the trail splits again at 0.7 mile. Continue hiking left (southwest) onto the loop portion of the trail to travel in a clockwise fashion. Hike west along Bashore Ridge and take in the views of South Blackburn Hollow to the south. Reach a trail junction at 2.0 miles where a spur trail leads to the Beaver Lake overlook.

Turn left (northwest) to follow the blue blazes out to Beaver Lake and take in the views at the overlook at 2.2 miles. Return via the same route to the main trail at 2.4 miles and turn left (northeast) back onto the Bashore Ridge Loop Trail. The trail travels northeast for just a short distance before it turns southeast to travel back down along Bashore Ridge. Reach the end of the loop portion of the hike at 3.7 miles. Turn left (northeast) to return to the Hidden Diversity Multi-Use Trailhead and parking area at 4.3 miles.

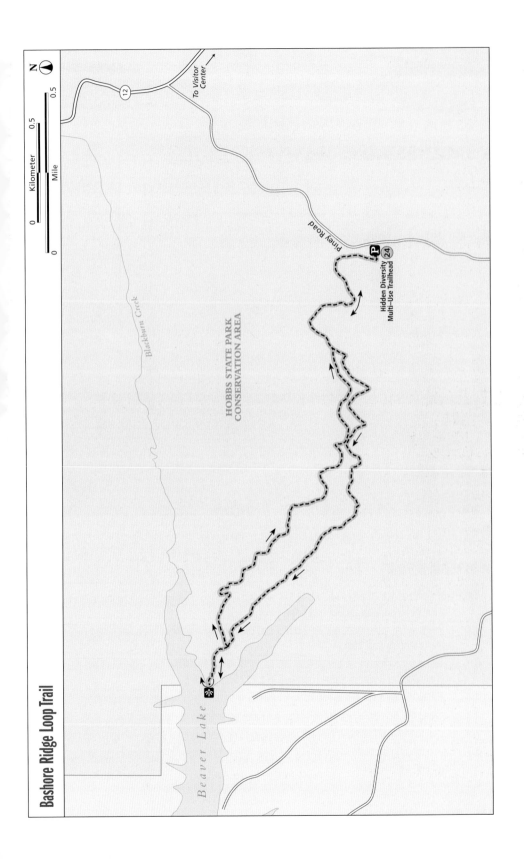

Bashore Ridge Loop Trail

Beaver Lake

Miles and Directions

0.0 From the Hidden Diversity Multi-Use Trail parking area and trailhead, begin hiking north on the Bashore Ridge Loop/Dutton Hollow Trails.

0.6 Come to a trail junction. Stay left (southwest) on the Bashore Ridge Loop Trail. Right (west) is the Dutton Hollow Trail.

0.7 Reach a second fork in the trail. Stay left (southwest) to begin the loop portion of the hike and to hike the Bashore Ridge Loop Trail in a clockwise fashion.

2.0 Come to the Beaver Lake overlook trail. Turn left (northwest) to hike to the overlook.

2.2 Arrive at the Beaver Lake overlook area. Turn around to return to the main trail.

2.4 Return to the main trail and turn left (northeast) to continue on the Bashore Ridge Loop Trail.

3.7 Reach the end of the loop portion of the hike. Turn left (northeast) to return to the trailhead and parking area.

4.3 Arrive back at the Hidden Diversity Multi-Use Trailhead and parking area.

25 Buffalo National River: Lost Valley Trail

One of the most popular trails in the area, the Lost Valley Trail offers year-round scenic beauty. An easy day hike in the upper district of the Buffalo National River takes you to Eden Falls. Highlights include the waterfall and a box canyon, bluff shelter, cave, and another waterfall within the cave.

Start: Lost Valley picnic and trailhead parking area
Distance: 2.4 miles out and back with small loop
Hiking time: About 2 hours
Difficulty: Easy due to length and small elevation gains
Trail surface: Forested trail, gravel, rock
Best season: Any

Other trail users: Hikers only
Canine compatibility: No dogs permitted
Schedule: Open year-round
Fees and permits: None
Maps: USGS Harrison
Trail contacts: Buffalo National River, 402 N. Walnut, Suite 136, Harrison, AR 72601; Pruitt Ranger Station (801) 446-5373; www.nps.gov/buff; emergency dispatch (888) 692-1162

Finding the trailhead: From Ponca, drive south on AR 43 for 1.4 miles. Turn right on Lost Valley Road and drive 0.5 mile to the picnic and trailhead parking area. GPS: N36 00.616' / W93 22.471'

The Hike

This is one of the most beautiful hikes in the state of Arkansas. It has so much packed into its relatively short mileage, you'll be awed at almost every bend in the trail. Not many 2.4-mile trails lead you to a natural bridge, two caves, and three waterfalls. Not surprisingly, the trail is incredibly popular, particularly on the weekends. If possible, visit on a weekday. The trail is accessible almost all year but is particularly nice in the early spring. Eden Falls is most impressive after a good rain. The trail also has plenty of interesting flora to examine. Look for columbine, toothwort, green trillium, and violet wood sorrel as you hike along the trail.

From the picnic and parking area, locate the Lost Valley Trailhead on the northwest end of the parking area. Begin hiking northwest on the wheelchair-accessible portion of the Lost Valley Trail. Along this section of the hike, the trail is level and well maintained. There are several benches available for anyone wanting to take a break, enjoy the natural beauty of the area, watch for wildlife, or listen for the Boxley Valley elk bugle during the fall rutting season.

At 0.7 mile the crushed-gravel, wheelchair-accessible portion of the trail comes to an end at a fork in the trail. Stay right (north) to hike along Clark Creek and visit the natural bridge, Cobb Cave, and Eden Falls. The trail to the left is the return trail.

Eden Falls

At 0.8 mile you'll reach the natural bridge. A small waterfall shoots out of a tunnel in the bridge, creating a beautiful pool at the base of the bridge.

Just past the natural bridge, come to another fork in the trail at 0.9 mile. Stay right to visit Cobb Cave and Eden Falls. At 1.0 mile reach another fork in the trail. Stay right and visit Cobb Cave, which is actually more of a bluff shelter than a cave. It is believed that Native Americans in the area once used Cobb Cave as a shelter. Just past Cobb Cave you'll come to the stunning Eden Falls. The 55-foot waterfall cascades down the mossy bluff into a blue-hued pool before flowing into Clark Creek.

Lost Valley Trail

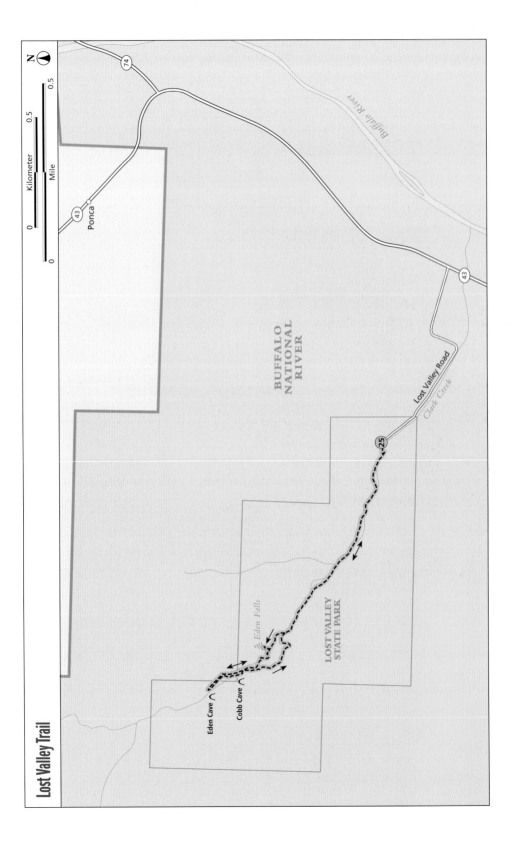

After relaxing and exploring this area, return to the trail and follow it as it climbs to the top of Eden Falls and the mouth of Eden Cave at 1.2 miles. Once in the mouth of the cave, you will need a flashlight/headlamp and a sense of adventure to go much farther. Assuming you have both, walk, crouch, and crawl the next 50 yards through the increasingly tight and dark corridor, which ends in a large room that contains another 35-foot waterfall. Take the opportunity to appreciate just how little light reaches this room by turning off your light for a moment. After exploring the cave and waterfall, make your way out of Eden Cave via the same route.

Now on the return portion of the hike, stay right at all forks in the trail, hiking above Clark Creek. The lollipop portion of the hike ends at 1.7 miles. Stay right, again walking on the wheelchair-accessible portion of the trail. Reach the trailhead and parking/picnic area at 2.4 miles.

Miles and Directions

0.0 Begin hiking northwest on the Lost Valley Trail.

0.7 The wheelchair-accessible portion of the trail ends. Stay right (north) at the fork.

0.8 Come to natural bridge.

0.9 At the fork in the trail, turn right (east) to visit Eden Falls and Cobb Cave.

1.0 The trail forks again. Stay right to and come to Cobb Cave. Reach the base of Eden Falls just past Cobb Cave. The trail climbs to Eden Cave just at the falls.

1.2 Enter Eden Cave and make your way through the narrow corridor. After about 50 yards come to the waterfall room. Leave the cave via same route.

1.4 Stay right (south) at the fork in the trail.

1.5 Stay right (south) at the fork in the trail.

1.7 End the lollipop portion of the hike. Stay right (southeast) to return to the trailhead.

2.4 Arrive back at the trailhead.

26 Buffalo National River: Centerpoint Trailhead to Hemmed-In Hollow

This 10.6-mile out-and-back hike in the Buffalo National River area has a little bit of everything that the Ozarks have to offer. Hikers choosing this route to Hemmed-In Hollow not only get to see the tallest waterfall between the Rockies and Appalachians, they will also have the opportunity to travel to one of the most scenic bluff overlooks that the river has to offer in Big Bluff. A visit to the Buffalo River, and a couple of river crossings, wrap up the highlights of this not-to-be-missed hike.

Start: Centerpoint Trailhead and parking area off AR 43

Distance: 10.6 miles out and back

Hiking time: About 5 to 6 hours

Difficulty: More challenging due to length and elevation changes

Trail surface: Forested path, dirt trail, river crossings

Best season: Best in late spring and fall for cooler temperatures

Other trail users: Bikers and equestrians

Canine compatibility: No dogs permitted

Fees and permits: None

Schedule: Open year-round

Maps: USGS Ponca; *National Geographic Trails Illustrated Map – Buffalo National River West (#232)*

Trail contacts: Buffalo National River, 402 N. Walnut, Suite 136, Harrison, AR 72601; (870) 365-2700; www.nps.gov/buff

Finding the trailhead: From Ponca, Arkansas, drive 3.5 miles north on AR 43 to the Centerpoint Trailhead and parking area on the right (east). GPS: N36 03.844' / W93 21.609'

The Hike

Get ready for an adventure on this hike! The Centerpoint Trail to Hemmed-In Hollow route includes the tallest sheer bluff between the Rockies and the Appalachians, two Buffalo National River crossings, and a visit to the tallest waterfall between the Rockies and the Appalachians. Big Bluff is considered by many Buffalo River fans as one of the most scenic spots to visit along the river. Towering at over 550 feet above the river, the bluff is a very noticeable landmark while paddling the river down below. Those who choose to hike to Big Bluff are in for a real treat. A small side trail known as the Goat Trail leads from the commonly used Centerpoint Trail and takes hikers out to experience Big Bluff up close and personal. The Goat Trail is a narrow path that leads out along the bluff and allows hikers to stand high above the Buffalo River. The trail supposedly gets its name from goats that escaped captivity from early settlers and eventually became wild. Many years ago visitors to the area would see the goats out on the bluff, hence the name the Goat Trail. Goats have not been seen out on the bluff for some time now, but the name has stuck.

A couple things to know before you make this trip: First, the best time to visit the bluff for photos is around three o'clock in the afternoon. The lighting is just right and makes for some beautiful photos of the bluff and surrounding views. Second, it is very important to watch your step and monitor children very closely on this section of trail, as there are extremely exposed parts. Most people would even recommend leaving small children at home for this one. The round-trip mileage from Centerpoint Trailhead to Big Bluff and back alone is 6.2 miles and may not be a suitable distance for small children anyway. Last, if you know you have an extreme fear of heights or vertigo issues, the side trip out to Big Bluff may not be for you. There is a nice place to wait for the others in your group at the beginning of the side trail though, so don't think you can't come along at all.

Locate the Centerpoint Trail and kiosk on the east side of the Centerpoint Trailhead and parking area and begin hiking east on the fairly wide trail. At just 0.2 mile you will come to a trail junction with the Chimney Rock Trail to the right (south). Stay left (east) on the Centerpoint Trail and continue hiking, as the trail will begin a gradual descent. This section of trail tends to have some rocky and rutted-up parts, as it is a multiuse trail. At 2.7 miles the trail levels out onto a saddle, an area that many people use as a resting and snacking spot, and you will see the Goat Trail junction off to the right (south). The Goat Trail is not marked except for a small sign down the trail just a bit that reads FOOT TRAFFIC ONLY. Continue down the Goat Trail as it becomes rocky and rugged and eventually makes its way out onto a small ledge that takes you out to Big Bluff at 3.1 miles. After a little exploring and some photos, return to the Centerpoint Trail at 3.5 miles and turn right (east) to continue downhill toward the Buffalo River.

As you reach the bottom of the valley, you will come to a trail junction with Sneeds Creek Trail at 4.3 miles. Turn right (east) onto Sneeds Creek Trail for a just a short distance until you reach another trail junction with the Old River Trail at 4.4 miles. Make a left (northeast) onto the Old River Trail and begin hiking along the Buffalo River. Not long after the Compton Trail intersects the Old River Trail from the left (west) at 4.6 miles, you will come to the first of two river crossings at 4.7 miles. More than likely your feet are going to get wet! Cross the river and easily pick the trail back up on the other side. Continue hiking northeast along the Old River Trail for a short distance to Horseshoe Bend at 4.8 miles, a very noticeable horseshoe-shaped turn in the trail. At the bend, turn left (north) onto the Hemmed-In Hollow Trail and prepare for your next river crossing at 4.9 miles. Cross the river and pick up the trail on the other side as it heads up into the forest along a stream.

Reach the final trail junction on the way to Hemmed-In Hollow at 5.5 miles. Stay right (northeast) to continue to the falls; left (southwest) leads to the Compton

Goat Trail overlooking Buffalo River Valley

Centerpoint Trailhead to Hemmed-In Hollow

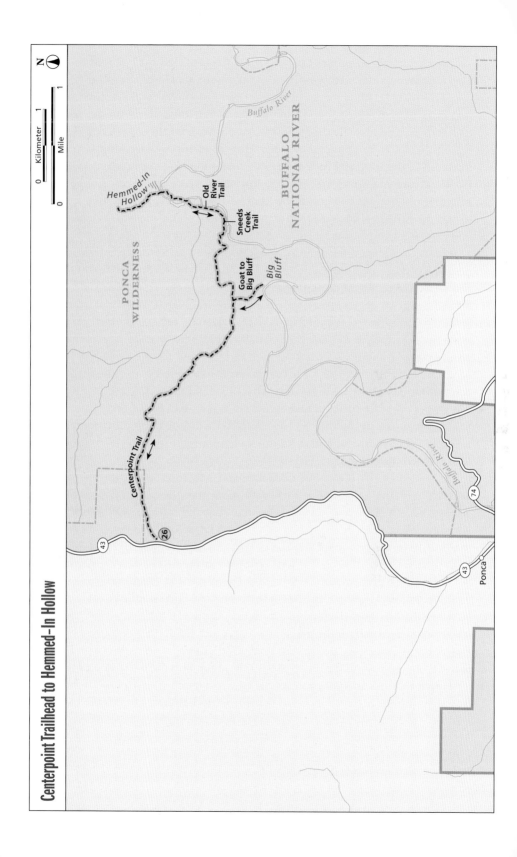

Trailhead. Arrive at Hemmed-In Hollow and the waterfall at 5.7 miles. Return to the Centerpoint Trailhead and parking area via the same route at 10.6 miles.

Miles and Directions

0.0 Locate the Centerpoint Trail on the east side of the Centerpoint Trailhead and parking area and begin hiking east on the trail.

0.2 Stay left (east) at the trail junction. Right (south) is the Chimney Rock Trail.

2.7 Arrive at a saddle and a trail junction. The Centerpoint Trail continues left (east), which is where you will return and continue after a short trip out to Big Bluff. Turn right (south) onto the unsigned Goat Trail.

3.1 Come to the scenic Big Bluff overlook.

3.5 Return to the Centerpoint Trail and turn right (east) to continue toward the Buffalo River and Hemmed-In Hollow.

4.3 Come to a trail junction with the Sneeds Creek Trail. Turn left (east) onto the Sneeds Creek Trail.

4.4 Reach another trail junction. Turn left (northeast) onto the Old River Trail.

4.6 The Compton Trail intersects the Old River Trail from the left (west). Continue right (northeast) on the Old River Trail.

4.7 The trail crosses the Buffalo River.

4.8 Arrive at Horseshoe Bend. Turn left (north) onto the Hemmed-In Hollow Trail.

4.9 Cross the Buffalo River.

5.5 Come to a trail junction and turn right (northeast) to stay on the Hemmed-In Hollow Trail.

5.7 Arrive at Hemmed-In Hollow.

10.6 Arrive back at the Centerpoint Trailhead and parking area.

27 Buffalo National River: Compton Trailhead to Hemmed-In Hollow

Follow this out-and-back trail to the tallest waterfall in the Ozarks. While Hemmed-In Hollow Waterfall flows year-round, the 210-foot waterfall is most impressive after a period of consistent rainfall. Early spring, after heavy summer storms, and fall tend to be the best times for maximum water flows. Spring and fall are particularly ideal due to cooler temperatures and either spring wildflowers or fall foliage.

Start: Compton Trailhead parking area
Distance: 5.0 miles out and back
Hiking time: About 4 hours or more
Difficulty: Difficult due to terrain
Trail surface: Forested trail
Best season: Best in spring and fall for cooler temperatures and likelihood of more water flowing at the falls
Other trail users: Bikers and equestrians

Canine compatibility: No dogs permitted
Fees and permits: None
Schedule: Open year-round
Maps: USGS Ponca; National Geographic Trails Illustrated Map – Buffalo National River West (#232)
Trail contacts: Buffalo National River, 402 N. Walnut, Suite 136, Harrison, AR 72601; (870) 365-2700; www.nps.gov/buff

Finding the trailhead: From Harrison, follow AR 43 south to Compton. Follow signs first to the Buffalo National River access road and then to the trailhead. GPS: N36 04.855' / W93 18.195'

The Hike

There is no doubt that Hemmed-In Hollow is a special place. Nestled in the heart of the Arkansas Ozarks, Hemmed-In Hollow is surrounded by the Ponca Wilderness Area. The 11,300-acre Ponca Wilderness Area is known for its rough terrain as well as its abundance of scenic wonders that include towering bluffs, scenic waterfalls, curious caves and cave-like formations, and clear mountain streams and springs.

There are several options for hiking to Hemmed-In Hollow Waterfall. Two access trails lead up from the Buffalo River. These are perhaps the "easiest" routes, but you will need a canoe or kayak to reach the trailheads. Hiking from the Centerpoint Trailhead provides a much longer and more challenging route. The 10.6-mile trip makes for a very long day hike or a shorter backpacking trip. Each of these options offers a totally unique experience.

The route detailed here is the Hemmed-In Hollow Trail from the Compton Trailhead. This is the most direct route for those traveling solely on foot. The 5.0-mile out-and-back trail is strenuous and may take much longer than 4 hours to complete

Compton Trailhead

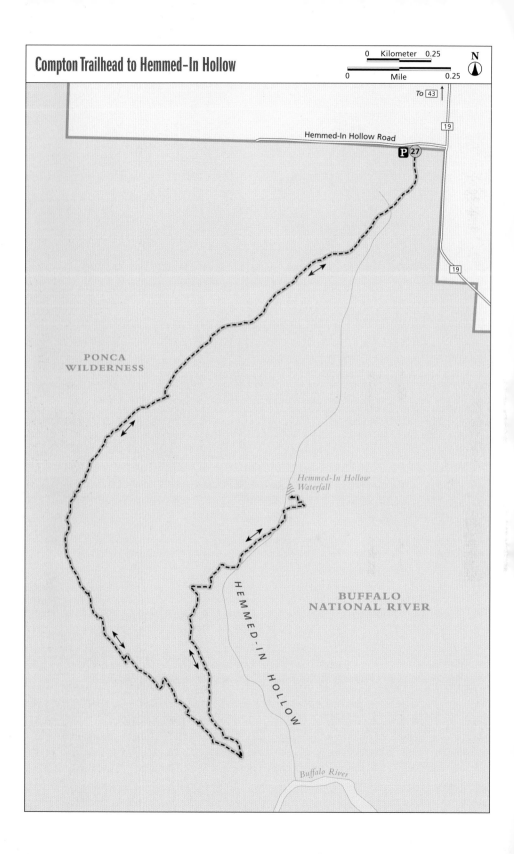

Compton Trailhead to Hemmed-In Hollow

0   Kilometer   0.25

0   Mile   0.25

N

To 43

19

Hemmed-In Hollow Road

P 27

19

PONCA
WILDERNESS

Hemmed-In Hollow
Waterfall

BUFFALO
NATIONAL RIVER

HEMMED-IN HOLLOW

Buffalo River

Hemmed-In Falls

depending on one's level of physical fitness and how long one chooses to linger at the waterfall. This trail is probably not a good choice for most young children. The trail descends nearly 1,500 feet from the Compton Trailhead to its lowest point, and the return trip is all uphill. Bring plenty of water and food, as you will likely need more than you usually would for a 5-mile trek. That being said, the prize is well worth the effort. As the trail descends into the steep valley, you are treated to some good views, a beautiful dense forest, curious rock formations, and a few smaller waterfalls. Despite its difficulty, the trail is quite popular, particularly on weekends. Visit on the weekdays

and there's a good chance you'll have the falls mostly to yourself. The hike ends at the tallest waterfall between the Appalachian and Rocky Mountains. Some 200-plus feet in height, Hemmed-In Falls is quite a sight. Even without the waterfall, the bluff it flows off of would be worth the hike.

There are two trails that leave from the Compton Trailhead: the Sneeds Creek Trail and the Hemmed-In Hollow Trail. The Hemmed-In Hollow Trail is signed not with this name but Ponca Wilderness Area/Falls Overlook/Hemmed-In Falls/ Buffalo River. Once there, it is pretty obvious which trail to take, but just in case, the Hemmed-In Hollow Trailhead is located east of the Sneeds Creek Trailhead. From the Compton Trailhead, begin hiking southwest on the Hemmed-In Hollow Trail.

At 0.8 mile come to the intersection with the Bench Trail and continue straight (southwest) on the Hemmed-In Hollow Trail. The trail from here is pretty straight-forward and fairly steep as it descends through the hardwood forest toward the Buf-falo River. During late fall, winter, and early spring, you will get some good views of the Buffalo River Valley and surrounding Ozarks.

Come to a fork in the trail at 1.8 miles. Stay left (northwest) to visit Hemmed-In Hollow Waterfall. The trail to the right (south) leads to the Buffalo River after about 1 mile and could make a nice side trip for those looking to extend their mileage. At 2.3 miles another trail merges with the Hemmed-In Hollow Trail from the right (south). This half-mile trail also leads to the Buffalo River. Continue northeast to Hemmed-In Hollow Waterfall.

Come to Hemmed-In Hollow Waterfall at 2.5 miles. After thoroughly enjoying the area, get ready to climb and return to the trailhead via the same route. At 5.0 miles arrive back at the Compton Trailhead.

Miles and Directions

0.0 From the Compton Trailhead, hike south on the Hemmed-In Hollow Trail marked for Ponca Wilderness Area/Falls Overlook/Hemmed-In Falls/Buffalo River.

0.8 At the intersection with the Bench Trail, continue straight (southwest).

1.8 Stay left (northwest) at the fork to visit Hemmed-In Hollow Waterfall.

2.3 Another trail merges from the right (south). Continue northeast to Hemmed-In Hollow Waterfall.

2.5 Come to Hemmed-In Hollow Waterfall. Return to Compton Trailhead via the same route.

5.0 Arrive back at the Compton Trailhead.

28 Ozark National Forest: Whitaker Point Trail

It's not hard to see why the 3.0-mile Whitaker Point Trail is one of the most popular hikes in Arkansas. Traversing through a gorgeous hardwood forest, the trail ultimately leads to Whitaker Point. This picturesque location offers gorgeous views of the Ozark Mountains, has been the setting for many a photo, and has served as the backdrop for several Arkansas tourism publications.

Start: From the Whitaker Point Trailhead
Distance: 3.0 miles out and back
Hiking time: About 2 hours
Difficulty: Moderate due to length
Trail surface: Forested path
Best season: Any
Other trail users: Hikers only
Canine compatibility: Leashed dogs permitted
Fees and permits: None

Schedule: Open year-round
Maps: USGS Boxley
Trail contacts: Ozark National Forest, Upper Buffalo Wilderness, Big Piney Ranger District–Jasper Office, PO Box 76, Highway 7 North, Jasper, AR 72641; (870) 446-5122; www .fs.usda.gov/main/osfnf/home. In case of emergency, contact the Newton County Sheriff at (870) 446-5124.

Finding the trailhead: From Ponca, drive south on AR 43 to AR 21. Turn left (south) onto AR 21 and go 1.2 miles toward the Boxley Bridge. Just before the bridge, turn right onto the unmarked Cave Mountain Road/CR 5. This steep, dirt road climbs Cave Mountain for 5.8 miles to the signed turnoff for the Hawksbill Trailhead, just past Cave Mountain Church. The parking area and trailhead are 0.2 mile down the gravel road. GPS: N35 53.891' / W93 27.479'

The Hike

The Arkansas Ozark region is a diverse area with steep, magnificent bluffs, dense forests, and abundant wildlife. Located along the northern edge of the Upper Buffalo Wilderness, the Whitaker Point Trail is one of the finest trails in the region and is sure to be a highlight of your time in the Ozark National Forest. The hiking trail is known by two different names: Hawksbill Crag Trail and Whitaker Point Trail. With bluffs that are well over 100 feet high, this 3.0-mile trail is an incredible place regardless of what you call it.

From the parking area, find the trail across the road (east). It is marked by a small stone monument honoring senator Dale Bumpers, who worked to protect wilderness areas like this one. Begin hiking east as the trail descends through the hardwood forest. At 0.1 mile come to a trail registration kiosk. Be sure to register as this helps land managers keep track of trail usage and also will help them find you in case of an emergency.

Cross a small drainage at 0.3 mile and continue downhill for a short distance. Several species of wildflowers flourish along the creek beds and bluff lines. Look for

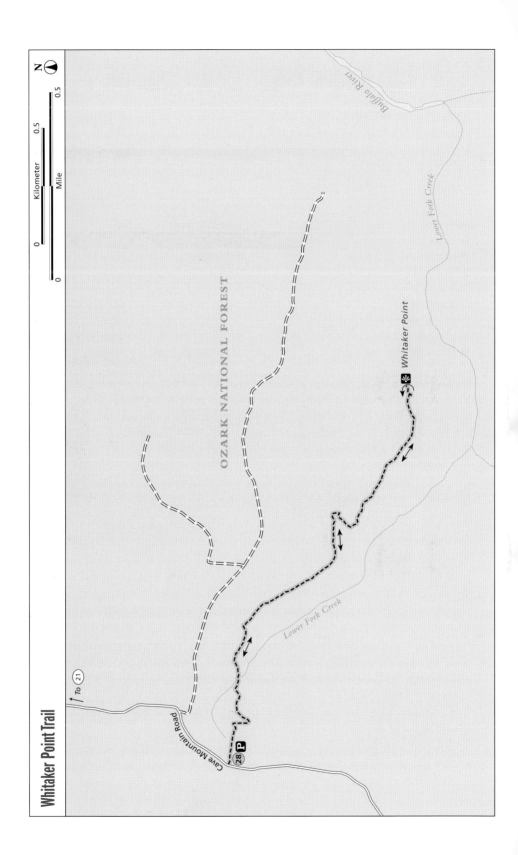

Whitaker Point Trail

N

0   Kilometer   0.5

0   Mile   0.5

To 21

Cave Mountain Road

28 P

Lower Fork Creek

Whitaker Point

OZARK NATIONAL FOREST

Lower Fork Creek

Buffalo River

View of Whitaker Point

rock geranium, sand flox, and shooting star. At 0.9-mile the trail crosses a small creek and then forks at an old road. Turn right (south) and follow the creek downstream a short distance to the edge of the bluff.

The trail turns left (southeast) at the bluff and follows it closely for the next 0.5 mile. This portion of the trail can be quite dangerous, so please use caution along the bluffs. Keep a close eye on children and pets as you explore the boulders and rock formations along the trail.

As the trail bends to the east, Whitaker Point (or Hawks Bill Brag) comes into view. There are several good photo opportunities here. Reach Whitaker Point at 1.5 miles. After snapping some photos and thoroughly enjoying the vista, return to the trailhead via the same route.

Miles and Directions

0.0 Begin hiking east on the Whitaker Point Trail.

0.1 Come to the registration kiosk.

0.3 Cross the creek and continue southeast.

0.9 Cross a creek again. Turn right (south), following the creek to the edge of the bluff.

1.5 Come to Whitaker Point. Return to the trailhead via the same route.

3.0 Arrive back at the trailhead.

29 Mount Magazine State Park: Bear Hollow Trail

The Bear Hollow Trail is a 5.6-mile out-and-back hike that travels along the upper rim of Bear Hollow. Considered some of the best scenery in the park, the Bear Hollow Trail offers access to Sunrise Rock and Inspiration Point. Both are popular places for nature lovers to come sit and take in beautiful sunrises in the morning or enjoy the peaceful sounds of nature in the evening.

Start: From the Benefield Picnic Area in Mount Magazine State Park

Distance: 5.6 miles out and back

Hiking time: About 3 to 4 hours

Difficulty: Moderate due to length

Trail surface: Forested path, dirt trail

Best season: Best in early spring and late fall for wildflowers and cooler temperatures

Other trail users: Equestrians

Canine compatibility: Leashed dogs permitted

Fees and permits: None

Schedule: Open year-round

Maps: USGS Blue Mountain; trail map available at the state park visitor center

Trail contacts: Mount Magazine State Park, 16878 Hwy. 309 S., Paris, AR 72855; (479) 963-8502; mountmagazinestatepark.com

Finding the trailhead: From Paris, Arkansas, drive south on AR 309 for 17.6 miles to the Benefield Picnic Area on the left (north). Turn into the picnic area and park at the Bear Hollow and Benefield Trailhead. GPS: N35 09.780' / W93 36.350'

The Hike

Topping out at 2,753 feet, Mt. Magazine has the distinction of being the highest point in the state of Arkansas. In the grand scheme of American mountains, Mt. Magazine may not seem like much of a challenge, but like much of the Ozarks, its beauty is in its nuances. Interesting geology, impressive displays of spring and summer wildflowers, and inspiring views of both the Ouachita Mountains and Ozarks Plateau make Mt. Magazine a nature-lover's dream.

With no geographic connection to another mountain, Mt. Magazine is home to several unique species of plants and animals. Each summer the park hosts the International Butterfly Festival, where visitors come to celebrate some to the state's most beautiful winged insects and hope to catch a glimpse of the extraordinary Diana Fritillary, an uncommon and particularly lovely species that calls Mt. Magazine home.

Mt. Magazine also offers a variety of activities for outdoor enthusiasts. In addition to hiking, the area is also used by mountain bikers, rock climbers, hang gliders, and equestrians. The park is a great place to spend a weekend, and the Bear Hollow Trail is a great starting point to explore this exceptional park.

Locate the Bear Hollow and Benefield Trailhead at the northern part of the Benefield Picnic Area parking lot. Begin hiking north on the trail and quickly encounter

Bear Hollow Trailhead

two trail junctions at 0.1 mile. Stay right (north) at the first junction toward the Bear Hollow and Benefield East Trails, and then stay left (northwest) at the second junction to continue on the Bear Hollow Trail. The trail travels high above Bear Hollow along the rim and offers amazing views of the Petit Jean Valley. Arrive at Sunrise Rock at 0.2 mile and continue hiking northwest to Inspiration Point at 0.4 mile. Not far past Inspiration Point, you will come to a trail junction at 0.5 mile. Stay right (west) on Bear Hollow Trail. Left (south) will take you to the Benefield West Loop Trail.

Once you've passed the Benefield West Loop Trail junction, the hiking is pretty smooth sailing, filled with great views and beautiful forests. The upper portions of Bear Hollow have never been logged and are believed to be some of the last remaining virgin hardwood in the state of Arkansas. At 1.2 miles you will cross Big Shoal Creek and then follow the trail as it turns east to hike around the northern rim of Bear Hollow. Continue along the northern rim until you reach the northern end of the Bear Hollow Trail at 2.8 miles. Turn around here and return to the Bear Hollow and Benefield Trailhead and parking area at 5.6 miles.

Bear Hollow Trail

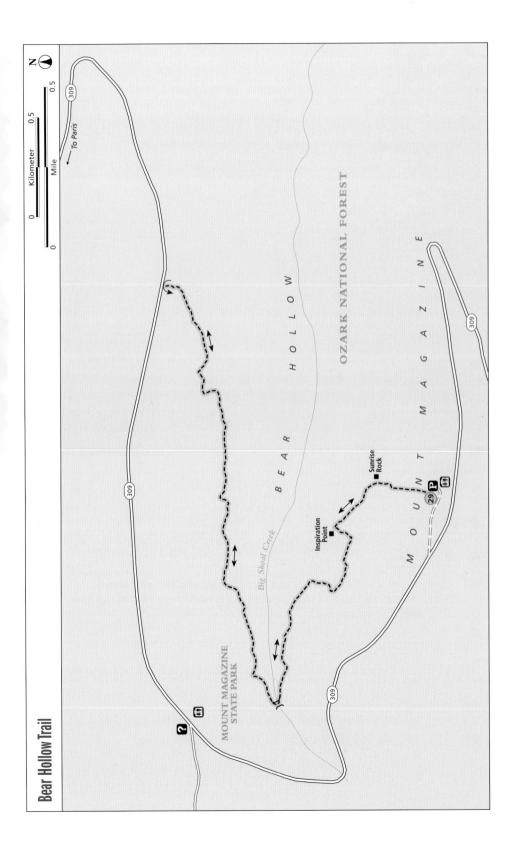

View from Bear Hollow Trail

Miles and Directions

0.0 Locate the Bear Hollow and Benefield Trailhead at the north part of the Benefield Picnic Area parking lot.

0.1 Stay right (north) on the Bear Hollow Trail/Benefield East Loop. Left (northwest) is the Benefield West Loop Trail. Then stay left (north) on the Bear Hollow Trail. Right (northeast) is the Benefield East Loop Trail.

0.2 Pass Sunrise Rock on the right (east).

0.4 Pass Inspiration Point on the right (north).

0.5 A trail to the left (south) connects hikers to the Benefield West Loop Trail. Stay right (west) on the Bear Hollow Trail.

1.2 Cross Big Shoal Creek and then cross through a glade.

2.8 Reach the northern end of the Bear Hollow Trail. Return to the trailhead and parking area.

5.6 Arrive back at the Bear Hollow and Benefield Trailhead and parking area.

30 Mount Magazine State Park: Highpoint Loop Trails

By connecting these four trails in Mount Magazine State Park, hikers have the opportunity to explore a large portion of Mount Magazine while knocking off a state highpoint at the same time. Signal Hill is Arkansas's highest point at 2,753 feet above sea level. The mountain is a retreat for many locals as the temperatures are a bit cooler in the summer as well as year-round. The unique habitat that is created here provides an ideal home for rare plants and animals.

Start: From the North Rim Trailhead just west of the Mount Magazine State Park Visitor Center
Distance: 5.5-mile loop
Hiking time: About 3 to 4 hours
Difficulty: Moderate due to length
Trail surface: Forested path, dirt trail, road crossings
Best season: Best in early spring and late fall for wildflowers and cooler temperatures

Other trail users: Hikers only
Canine compatibility: Leashed dogs permitted
Fees and permits: None
Schedule: Open year-round
Maps: USGS Blue Mountain; trail map available at the state park visitor center
Trail contacts: Mount Magazine State Park, 16878 Hwy. 309 S., Paris, AR 72855; (479) 963-8502; mountmagazinestatepark.com

Finding the trailhead: From Paris, Arkansas, drive south on AR 309 for 17.5 miles to the Mount Magazine State Park Visitor Center. Turn right (north) into the parking area and locate the trailhead at the west end of the parking lot. GPS: N35 10.730' / W93 36.950'

The Hike

Mount Magazine State Park is home to the highest point in the state of Arkansas. For those not familiar, many people take part every year in checking off state highpoints from their personal to-do lists. Those that take part on a regular basis simply call it "highpointing." As you can imagine, getting to each state's summit is going to be a different experience each time. A trip to Florida's highpoint, the lowest in elevation of the fifty states, simply requires that you drive to the destination and get out of the car next to the sign in a roadside park and snap a photo. To get to the highest state highpoint, Alaska's 20,320-foot Denali, requires a bit more effort and training. Much more about "highpointing" can be learned at the Highpointers Club website, highpointers.org. A list of the state highpoints, access issues and concerns, directions to trailheads, and even membership to the Highpointing Club can all be found here.

The Arkansas Highpoint on Mount Magazine, known as Signal Hill, is considered one of the easier highpoint hikes if you are simply hiking the Signal Hill Trail. Depending on your approach, the hike can be as short as 0.8-mile round-trip. The hike is a very gradual uphill climb from the parking area to a well-maintained highpoint. Very proud of its status as the highest point in Arkansas, Mount Magazine State

View from Highpoint Trail

Park has even developed a brochure just for your hike up to the highpoint. It is not uncommon to see a maintenance crew on the summit making sure that things are as they should be for hikers to enjoy their visit. A large stone map of Arkansas has been constructed at the summit right next to a wooden sign indicating that you have reached the summit. Many people come to the park, hike the summit trail, snap a few photos, and are on their way. This route to the highpoint connects four beautiful trails located in the park that make for an ideal half-day adventure.

Locate the North Rim Trailhead sign just west of the Mount Magazine State Park Visitor Center and begin hiking west on the trail. The North Rim Trail does just exactly as its name indicates, traveling along the north rim of Mount Magazine. It also offers spectacular views of the Ozark Mountains to the north. At 0.3 mile you will cross School Creek and then Dill Creek at 0.6 mile. Both creeks are small and easily crossed. Not far past Dill Creek, you will come to Dill Point at 0.8 mile. Dill Point is a great place to take in the scenery before continuing your hike as the trail turns southwest. At 1.8 miles turn left (south) to leave the North Rim Trail and head toward the Mossback Ridge and Signal Hill Trails. Cross the park road and then turn

Highpoint Loop Trails

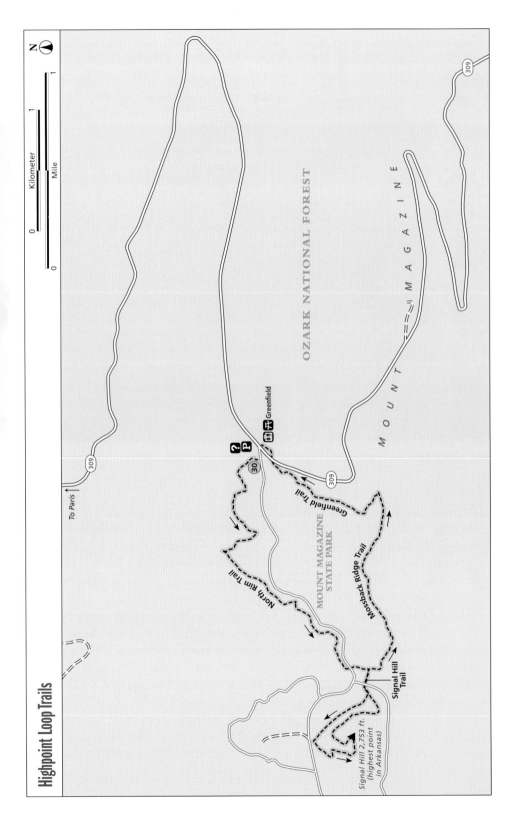

N

0   Kilometer   1
0   Mile   1

To Paris

309

OZARK NATIONAL FOREST

MOUNT MAGAZINE

MOUNT MAGAZINE STATE PARK

North Rim Trail

Greenfield Trail

Mossback Ridge Trail

Signal Hill Trail

Signal Hill 2,753 ft. (highest point in Arkansas)

Greenfield

309

30

The peak of Mount Magazine is the highest point in the state of Arkansas.

right (west) to head to the Signal Hill Trail and the Arkansas Highpoint at 1.9 miles. Cross the park road again at 2.0 miles and begin your approach to the highpoint on the Signal Hill Trail.

Just after crossing the road and beginning your hike on the Signal Hill Trail, turn right (northwest) to approach the highpoint from the north on the Signal Hill Trail. The highpoint trail is an excellent hike in the spring when the dogwood trees are in bloom. At 2.5 miles turn left (south) to continue the approach to the highpoint. Right (north) leads to a parking area and campground. Arrive at the highpoint at 2.9 miles. From the highpoint, descend back down the Signal Hill Trail as it leaves the highpoint headed north, turns east, and then south. At 3.3 miles turn left (east) to head back to the Mossback Ridge Trail and then stay right (northeast) at 3.4 miles to continue towards Mossback Ridge. You will cross the park road again at 3.5 miles and then turn right (south) onto the Mossback Ridge Trail at 3.6 miles. Much like the North Rim Trail, the Mossback Ridge Trail does just as its name might suggest. The trail climbs up and then travels east along Mossback Ridge. At 4.7 miles you will

reach a trail junction. Turn left (north) onto the Greenfield Trail. To the right (east) the Mossback Ridge Trail continues. Hike north along the Greenfield Trail and cross the Big Shoal Creek at 4.8 miles. The trail descends down off of Mossback Ridge and eventually crosses the AR 309 at 5.4 miles.

After crossing the road and continuing northeast, you will reach the Greenfield Picnic Area and the end of the loop at 5.45 miles. You can return to the parking area and trailhead just across the highway to the northwest. Return to the trailhead at 5.5 miles.

Miles and Directions

0.0   Locate the North Rim Trailhead just west of the Mount Magazine State Park Visitor Center and begin hiking west.

0.3   Cross School Creek.

0.6   Cross Dill Creek.

0.8   Come to Dill Point on the right (north).

1.8   Turn left (south) toward the Mossback Ridge Trail and then cross the park road.

1.9   Turn right (west) toward the Signal Hill Trail.

2.0   Cross the park road and begin hiking west on the Signal Hill Trail toward the highest point in Arkansas.

2.1   Make a right (northwest) to approach the highpoint from the north.

2.5   Turn left (south) for the final approach to the highpoint. Right (north) leads to a parking area and the campground.

2.9   Arrive at the Arkansas Highpoint.

3.3   Turn left (east) to head back to the Mossback Ridge Trail. Right (west) goes to the Lodge.

3.4   Stay right (northeast) to continue toward the Mossback Ridge Trail. Left (north) goes back onto the Signal Hill Trail.

3.5   Cross the park road.

3.6   Turn right (south) onto the Mossback Ridge Trail.

4.7   Turn left (north) onto the Greenfield Trail.

4.8   Cross Big Shoal Creek.

5.4   Cross the park road.

5.4   Come to the Greenfield Picnic Area and cross the road to the trailhead.

5.5   Return to the North Rim Trailhead and parking area.

31 Mount Nebo State Park: Bench Road Trail

Located near Dardanelle, this interesting and easy day hike circles Mount Nebo State Park on a forested path that was once an old wagon road. A perfect choice for a lunch-break day hike, a short weekend stroll, or a quick escape from the city, this hike passes several springs and ventures through a forest rich in bird- and other wildlife-viewing opportunities. The trail is mostly flat and offers good views from the mountain during late fall through early spring.

Start: From Bench Road Trailhead and Bench Overlook parking area
Distance: 4.0-mile loop
Hiking time: About 2 hours
Difficulty: Easy due to mostly level terrain
Trail surface: Old dirt road
Best season: Any
Other trail users: Hikers, mountain bikers, horseback riders

Canine compatibility: Leashed dogs permitted
Fees and permits: None
Schedule: Open year-round
Maps: USGS Chickalah Mountain East; trail map available at visitor center
Trail contacts: Mt. Nebo State Park, 16728 W. State Highway 155, Dardanelle, AR 72834; (479) 229-3655; moutnebo@arkansas.com; www.arkansasstateparks.com/mountnebo

Finding the trailhead: From Dardanelle, take AR 22 West. Turn left (west) on SH 155 for 5.5 miles. The parking area for the Bench Trail and Bench Overlook are on the right. GPS: N35 14.140' / W93 09.810'

The Hike

Like many of the state parks in Arkansas, Mount Nebo is a local gem. At 1,350 feet, Mount Nebo offers visitors great views of the Arkansas River Valley, Lake Dardanelle, and the surrounding Ozark topography. It is typically 10° to 15°F cooler atop Mount Nebo, so it also makes a great escape during warmer weather. The state park has an interesting history, dating back to its existence as a pre–Civil War era vacation destination; it offers visitors a glimpse into what Ozark resort life looked like during the late 1800s. During the 1890s a luxury resort called the Summit Park Hotel was constructed here to appeal to steamboat passengers on the Arkansas River. The summertime guests enjoyed the same natural beauty that continues to attract visitors to the mountain. The hotel burned in 1918.

Part of the mountain was designated an Arkansas state park in 1927. Soon after that, the stock market crash of 1929 skyrocketed the US unemployment rate to 23 percent. In 1933, with nearly a quarter of the American workforce unemployed, Franklin D. Roosevelt proposed New Deal legislation that led to the creation of the

Bench Road Trail ▷

View from Bench Road Trail Overlook

Civilian Conservation Corps (CCC). By July of 1933 a CCC company was beginning work at Mount Nebo State Park. Using rocks and trees from Mount Nebo, the CCC built many of the structures found here today, including most of the trails, bridges, cabins, and pavilions.

In many ways the state park still feels a bit like a resort today. In addition to the rustic CCC cabins, the park offers modern amenities including contemporary cabins, a swimming pool, tennis court, playground, bike rentals, and a visitor center. The park's 14 miles of trails give hikers the opportunity to enjoy the natural and historical significance of Mount Nebo. Deer, raccoons, opossums, and other Ozark critters are likely to be spotted along any of the trails in the park. Bench Road Trail is an excellent choice because it visits many of the park's historical areas and connects with every other trail in the park, giving hikers the opportunity to extend this hike as much as they would like.

The Bench Road Trailhead is located just north of the Bench Overlook shelter. A narrow sandstone shelf, also called a bench, encircles the mountain about 300 feet

Bench Road Trail

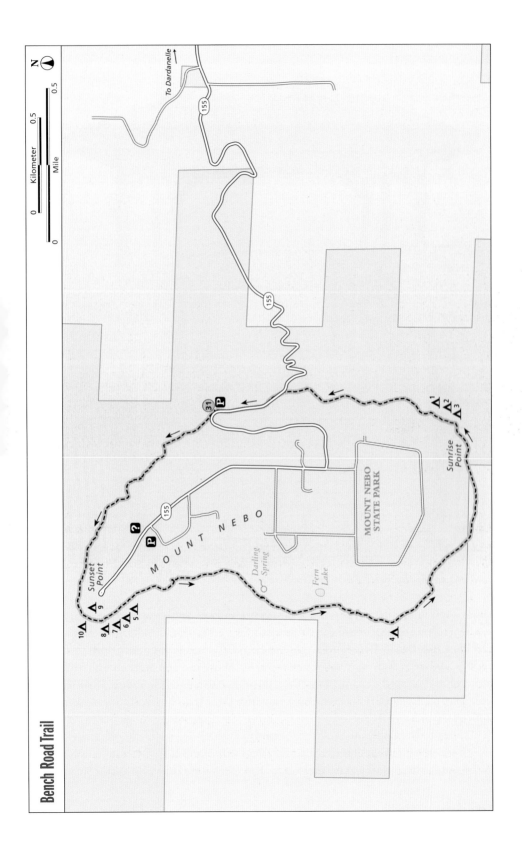

Bench Overlook near Bench Road Trail Trailhead

below the summit. The bench is actually part of a large sandstone slab. Erosion has exposed the outer edge of the slab and created the visible bench. In the 1890s this trail was known as Bench Boulevard and led to Fern Lake, a hotel, homes, a store, several springs, and steps that were a part of the resort. Many of these areas are still visible from the trail today. The "Miles and Directions" below are for the Bench Road Trail only. Trail intersections and descriptions to where those trails lead will add length and difficulty to this hike.

From the Bench Road Trailhead, begin hiking northwest on the old dirt road. At 0.3 mile come to the intersection with the Nebo Springs Trail. If you follow the Nebo Springs Trail to the right (east), it leads a very short distance to Nebo Springs,

a moss-covered spring used by the earliest residents of Mount Nebo. Continue south on the Bench Road Trail.

At 0.4 mile come to the intersection with the Nebo Steps Trail, which leads west, up the mountain to the Rim Trail and Visitor Center. Continue northwest along Bench Road Trail. Come to the spur trail for the Bench Road Trail Campsites 5 through 10 at 1.0 mile and continue south along the Bench Road Trail.

The stairs leading to Darling Springs are located at 1.3 miles. During the late 1800s guests of the resort would visit and relax at the gazebos located here and at Gum Springs. A trail to Campsites 5 through 10 is found to the right (west) side of the Bench Road Trail. Continue south on the Bench Road Trail.

At 1.7 miles pass between Crystal/Lion Springs on the right (west) and Fern Lake on the left (east). Near Fern Lake is a spur trail that connects to the 1.0-mile loop of Summit Park Trail. Continue hiking south on the Bench Road Trail.

Pass Group Camp 4, Gum Springs Trail, and Gum Springs at 2.0 miles. Continue south on the Bench Road Trail, passing Campsites 1 through 3 at 3.0 miles.

Reach the intersection with the Varnall Springs Trail at 3.3 miles. Varnall Springs is located about 0.25 mile to the east on the Varnall Springs Trail. Continue north to stay on the Bench Road Trail. At 3.6 miles the trail comes to the parking area for the hike-in campsites located along Bench Road Trail. Turn left (northwest) here and hike along SH 155. Return to the Bench Overlook and Bench Road Trail parking area at 4.0 miles.

Miles and Directions

0.0 From the Bench Overlook and Bench Road Trail parking area, begin hiking northwest on the old dirt road.

0.3 At the intersection with the Nebo Springs Trail, continue northwest along the old road.

0.4 At the intersection with the Nebo Steps Trail, continue northwest.

1.0 Come to the turnoff for Bench Road Trail Campsites 5 through 10 on the right (west) side of the trail. The trail to the left (east) leads to the visitor center. Continue south on Bench Road Trail.

1.3 Darling Springs is to the left (east) side of trail. The trail to Campsites 5 through 10 is on the right (west) side of trail. Continue south on the Bench Road Trail.

1.7 Come to Crystal/Lion Springs on the right (west) side of the trail, Fern Lake on the left (east), and access to the Summit Park Trail. Continue south on Bench Road Trail.

2.0 Reach Group Camp 4 on the right (west) side of the trail and Gum Springs Trail on the left (east). Continue south on Bench Road Trail.

3.0 Come to Campsites 1 through 3 on the right (southeast) side of trail. Continue northeast on Bench Road Trail.

3.3 At the intersection with the Varnall Springs Trail, continue north on the Bench Road Trail.

3.6 Come to the parking area for hike-in campsites on the Bench Road Trail. Turn left (northwest) and hike along SH 155 to the Bench Overlook and Bench Road Trail parking area.

4.0 End the loop at the Bench Overlook and Bench Road Trail parking area.

32 Petit Jean State Park: Cedar Falls Trail

The Cedar Falls Trail is the most popular trail in the park. The trail travels 200 vertical feet down into Cedar Creek Canyon and then follows Cedar Creek north to Cedar Falls. The falls cascade more than 90 feet to the canyon floor and are a perfect escape for hikers looking to get away from the summer heat. Cedar Falls was added to the register of Arkansas Natural Areas back in 1977 and is a beautiful backdrop for lunch or a snack break.

Start: From the Cedar Falls Trailhead in Petit Jean State Park
Distance: 2.0 miles out and back
Hiking time: About 1 to 2 hours
Difficulty: Moderate due to elevation gain
Trail surface: Rocky trail, forested path, wooden footbridge
Best season: Year-round
Other trail users: Hikers only

Canine compatibility: Leashed dogs permitted
Fees and permits: None
Schedule: Open year-round
Maps: USGS Adona; trail map available at the visitor center
Trail contacts: Petit Jean State Park, 1285 Petit Jean Mountain Rd., Morrilton, AR 72110; (501) 727-5441; petitjeanstatepark.com

Finding the trailhead: From Morrilton, Arkansas, drive south on AR 9 for 5.6 miles and turn right (west) onto AR 154. Continue to 18.1 miles on AR 154 and then turn right (west) toward Mather Lodge. Arrive at the Mather Lodge parking area at 18.3 miles. Locate the Cedar Falls Trailhead behind the lodge on the west end. GPS: N35 07.030' / W92 56.330'

The Hike

President Franklin D. Roosevelt established the Civilian Conservation Corps (CCC) in 1933 as a way to get Americans working and earning money during the Great Depression. Many of the men in the CCC were World War I veterans with experience in construction. The CCC came in and worked at Petit Jean State Park from 1933 to 1938. Designated Arkansas's first state park in 1923, with the help of the CCC, Petit Jean soon became one of the most beautiful state parks in the country. The CCC first constructed living quarters for their camp and soon after, they built Mather Lodge and the surrounding cabins. Workers also constructed a stone dam to form Lake Bailey and a water tower to supply water to Mather Lodge and the cabins.

The CCC also spent time constructing roads, pavilions, and, of course, trails. The Cedar Falls area includes the first 80 acres that were originally designated as a state park. The trail was a grueling process as the crew carved a series of native stone steps down the 200-vertical-foot descent into Cedar Creek Canyon. After hiking the trail you will see that the end result was well worth the effort. When all was said and done, the work done by the CCC at Petit Jean State Park has been recognized as some of the outstanding examples of CCC work in Arkansas. Today, Petit Jean State Park has

View from Cedar Falls Trail

three National Historic Districts that include more than eighty buildings, structures, trails, and bridges.

Locate the Cedar Falls Trailhead behind Mather Lodge on the west end. Mather Lodge is the only CCC-constructed lodge in the Arkansas state park system. Begin hiking south on the trail and quickly come to a trail junction at 0.1 mile. Stay right (south) on the Cedar Falls Trail. Left (west) leads to the Bear Cave Area. From here, begin your steep descent down the stone stairs into Cedar Creek Canyon. You'll descend about 200 vertical feet in about 0.2 mile. Once on the canyon floor, you will come to a nicely constructed wooden footbridge at 0.4 mile. Cross the bridge and then turn right (north) to continue toward Cedar Falls. To the left (south) after crossing the bridge is the Canyon Trail.

Hike along Cedar Creek as the trail turns northeast and eventually east through the cool and quiet canyon. Arrive at Cedar Falls at 1.0 mile. The falls cascade over 90 feet into a beautiful pool of water that then flows through the surrounding boulders into Cedar Creek. From here, return to the Cedar Falls Trailhead via the same route at 2.0 miles.

Cedar Falls Trail

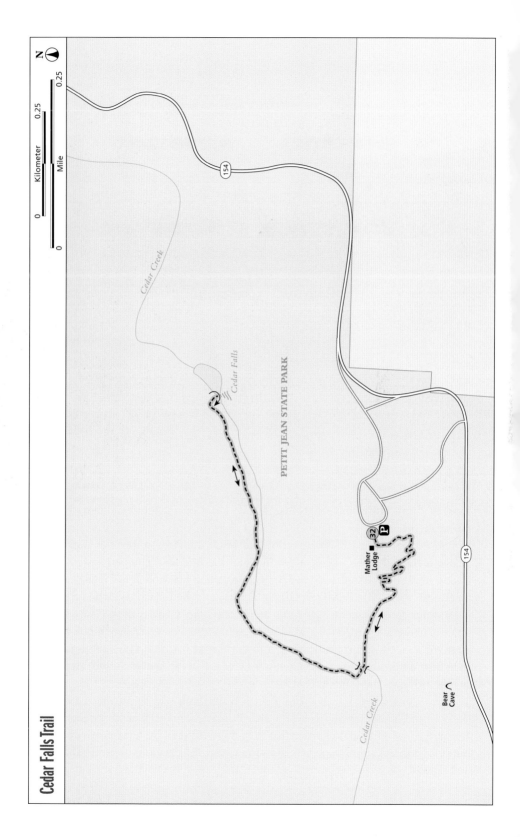

N

Kilometer
0   0.25   0.25
0   0.25
Mile

154

Cedar Creek

Cedar Falls

PETIT JEAN STATE PARK

Cedar Creek

Mather Lodge

32

P

154

Bear Cave

Cedar Falls

Miles and Directions

0.0   Locate the Cedar Falls Trailhead behind Mather Lodge at the western end.

0.1   Stay right (south) on the Cedar Falls Trail. Left (west) leads to the Bear Cave Area.

0.4   Cross a footbridge and then turn right (north) toward Cedar Falls. To the left (south) is the Canyon Trail.

1.0   Arrive at Cedar Falls.

2.0   Arrive back at the Cedar Falls Trailhead.

33 Petit Jean State Park: Seven Hollows Trail

The Seven Hollows Trail is one of many hiking gems in Petit Jean State Park. The loop trail travels in and out of a series of hollows and offers several highlights along the way. A natural bridge, a grotto, and large boulders that resemble turtle shells are the geologic features that accompany the beautiful landscape. The old-growth hardwood forest is a nature lover's dream and any rock hound will be thrilled to explore the area.

Start: From the Seven Hollows Trailhead in Petit Jean State Park
Distance: 4.1-mile loop
Hiking time: About 2 to 3 hours
Difficulty: Moderate due to length
Trail surface: Forested path, dirt trail
Best season: Early spring and late fall
Other trail users: Hikers only

Canine compatibility: Leashed dogs permitted
Fees and permits: None
Schedule: Open year-round
Maps: USGS Adona; trail map available at the visitor center
Trail contacts: Petit Jean State Park, 1285 Petit Jean Mountain Rd., Morrilton, AR 72110; (501) 727-5441; petitjeanstatepark.com

Finding the trailhead: From Morrilton, Arkansas, drive south on AR 9 for 5.6 miles and turn right (west) onto AR 154. Continue to 18.6 miles on AR 154 and then turn left (south) into the Seven Hollows Trail parking area. GPS: N35 06.870' / W92 56.730'

The Hike

The idea of Petit Jean Mountain becoming a recreation destination first started in 1907. A group of businessmen who were inspecting a logging mill wound up spending most of their time riding horseback and log trains through the valleys and over the mountain. They even explored the Seven Hollows region, all of which was owned by their company. The difficulties of logging the region were discussed at length. The men decided that any effort to log the area would come at a financial loss for the company. During their discussions one of the men even suggested that the area be offered to the federal government as a national park. The area actually went through several processes to be proposed as a national park but was eventually rejected because the area was thought to be too small considering the expense of development. However, the Park Service suggested that the area be brought to the state's attention to become a state park. After more paperwork and more proposals, the area was finally approved as Arkansas's first state park in 1923.

Locate the Seven Hollows Trailhead at the northwest corner of the parking area and begin hiking west. After just 0.1 mile you will reach the loop portion of the hike.

Natural bridge on Seven Hollows Trail ▷

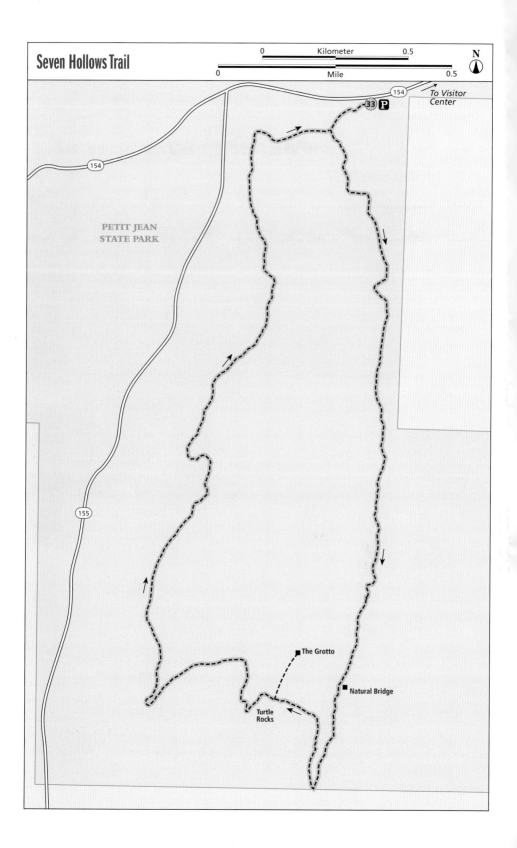

Seven Hollows Trail

0   Kilometer   0.5

0   Mile   0.5

N

154

33 P

To Visitor Center

154

PETIT JEAN STATE PARK

155

The Grotto

Natural Bridge

Turtle Rocks

Seven Hollows Trail

Turn left (southeast) to begin hiking the loop. As you hike and the trail begins dropping down into the first hollow, you will soon discover why logging crews were not interested in trying to come into the area back in the early 1900s. Access in and out of the area would have been a nightmare back then. After a few small creek crossings, you will arrive at the Natural Bridge on the left (east). Continue hiking south through the hollow as the trail dips down and crosses the creek a few more times. At 1.7 miles you will come to an area known as the Turtle Rocks. The name was given to large rocks in the area that look like turtle shells. Chemicals in rainwater slowly created all these veins that run through the rock to form this unusual design.

At 2.0 miles you will come to a spur trail that leads to the northeast and goes to a neat little box canyon called the Grotto. If you choose to visit the Grotto, hike 0.2 mile to the Grotto and then back to rejoin the main trail. Hike up out of the hollow and cross a glade before descending back down into the next hollow, where you will cross a small footbridge at 3.0 miles. This hollow becomes very wide and quite beautiful. As the hollow begins to narrow more, you will reach a trail junction where the Winthrop P. Rockefeller Boy Scout Trail intersects from the left (west). Stay right (north) to continue on the Seven Hollows Trail and eventually reach the end of the loop portion at 4.0 miles. Turn left (north) to return to the trailhead and the Seven Hollows parking area at 4.1 miles.

Prickly pear on Seven Hollows Trail

Miles and Directions

0.0 Locate the Seven Hollows Trailhead at the northwest corner of the parking area and begin hiking west.

0.1 Come to a trail junction and turn left (southeast) to begin the loop portion of the hike.

1.2 Arrive at the Natural Bridge on the left (east).

1.7 Pass an area known as the Turtle Rocks.

2.0 Reach a spur trail on the right (northeast) that leads to the Grotto.

3.0 Cross a small footbridge and begin traveling through a beautiful rocky hollow.

3.7 The Winthrop P. Rockefeller Boy Scout Trail intersects from the left (west). Stay right (north) to continue on the Seven Hollows Trail.

4.0 Reach the end of the loop portion of the hike. Turn left (north) to return to the trailhead and parking area.

4.1 Arrive back at the trailhead.

34 Ozark National Forest: Pedestal Rocks Trail

Pedestal Rocks Trail is one of the best trails in this Ozarks park. In addition to exploring the geologic wonders of the weathered limestone "pedestals," the remote area also offers caves, an abundance of wildlife and wildflowers, and spectacular views of the north fork of the Illinois Bayou. Hike the trail in October for the best chance to see the surrounding forest brightly adorned in fall colors.

Start: Trailhead and parking lot for Pedestal Rocks Scenic Area
Distance: 2.5-mile lollipop
Hiking time: About 2 hours
Difficulty: Moderate due to length and trail condition
Trail surface: Forested path and rock
Best season: Early fall through late spring
Other trail users: Hikers only

Canine compatibility: Leashed dogs permitted
Fees and permits: None
Schedule: Open year-round
Maps: USGS Sand Gap
Trail contacts: Ozark–St. Francis National Forests, Bayou Ranger District, 12000 SR 27, Hector, AR 72843; (479) 284-3150; www.fs.usda.gov/main/osfnf

Finding the trailhead: From Pelsor, Arkansas, take AR 16 for 5.9 miles to the turnoff for the Pedestal Rocks Scenic Area. Turn right and drive 0.1 mile to the parking area. GPS: N35 40.390' / W92 56.190'

The Hike

Found in the heart of the Ozarks, the Bayou Ranger District of the Ozark National Forest offers visitors beautiful views, towering bluffs, unusual rock formations, crystal-clear streams, and densely forested woodlands. The Pedestal Rocks Scenic Area has two trails, the Pedestal Rocks Trail and the King's Bluff Trail. This guide highlights the 2.2-mile Pedestal Rocks Trail, but one could easily extend this day hike by adding on the 1.7-mile King's Bluff Trail, which features a waterfall that is over 100 feet high. If you have the time and ability, the King's Bluff Trail is well worth your while. A vault toilet and several picnic benches are available near the parking area. Water is not available, however.

Like much of the Ozark's topography, the Pedestal Rocks Scenic Area owes its unique beauty to the power of erosion. The "pedestals" found on this trail are the result of thousands of years of weathering by water and wind. Also similar to the landscape of much of the Ozarks are the steep bluffs found near the pedestals. It is possible to find safe routes to scramble down to the base of the pedestals, but please use caution, especially if you are hiking with children. It would be very easy to lose footing along these bluffs and even a short fall could have a fatal outcome in this fairly remote area. In addition to natural beauty, the area also has historical significance. It is

View from Pedestal Rocks

believed that the prehistoric peoples that once inhabited the area used the caves and natural shelters here.

From the Pedestal Rocks Scenic Area parking lot, locate the small bridge to the south. Cross the bridge and come to the Pedestal Rocks and the King's Bluff Trailheads. Take the trail to the left (south) to hike the Pedestal Rocks Trail. Come to a trail intersection at 0.1 mile. The trail to the right (west) is the return trail for the King's Bluff Trail. The trail to the left (southeast) is the return trail for the Pedestal Rocks Trail. Continue southwest on the middle trail to hike the Pedestal Rocks Trail in a counterclockwise loop.

Pedestal Rocks Trail

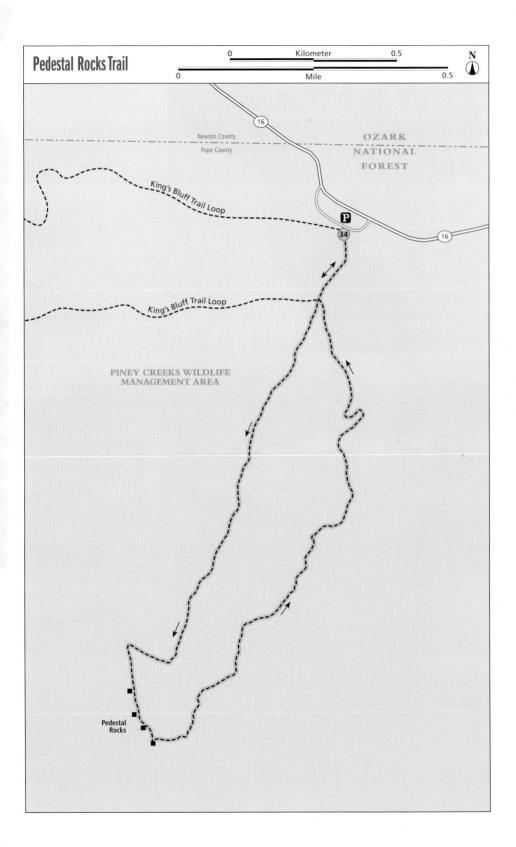

0   Kilometer   0.5

0   Mile   0.5

N

16

Newton County

Pope County

OZARK

NATIONAL

FOREST

King's Bluff Trail Loop

P

34

16

King's Bluff Trail Loop

PINEY CREEKS WILDLIFE
MANAGEMENT AREA

Pedestal
Rocks

The relatively flat trail traverses through a thick, mostly hardwood woodland for about a mile before descending to the bluff and Pedestal Rocks area at 1.1 miles. From here, the trail bends to the southeast, following the bluff line for about 0.5 mile. There are plenty of opportunities to explore the bluff in this area. Please use extreme caution and practice Leave No Trace guidelines by sticking to the designated trail.

At 1.7 miles come to a natural arch, marking the end of the Pedestal Rocks area. The trail bends to the east-northeast and passes a spring and small waterfall. Continue north-northeast on the Pedestal Rocks Trail, coming to the end of the loop at 2.4 miles. Turn right (north) and return to the Pedestal Rocks and King's Bluff Trailheads at 2.5 miles.

Miles and Directions

0.0 From the Pedestal Rocks Scenic Area parking lot, cross a small bridge to the Pedestal Rocks and King's Bluff Trailheads. Stay left (south) to hike the Pedestal Rocks Trail.

0.1 At the trail intersection, continue southwest on the middle trail.

1.1 Reach a bluff and Pedestal Rocks. Explore at will.

1.7 Come to an arch near the end of the Pedestal Rocks. The trail bends to the east-northeast and passes a spring and small waterfall.

2.0 Continue north-northeast on the Pedestal Rocks Trail.

2.4 End the loop portion of the hike and turn right (north).

2.5 Arrive back at the Pedestal Rocks and King's Bluff Trailheads.

Rock formation at Pedestal Rocks

35 Buffalo National River: Buffalo River Trail–Spring Creek Section

This 11.6-mile out-and-back section of the Buffalo River Trail passes over three towering bluffs that offer spectacular views of the river and the surrounding Ozark Mountains. While traveling along the top of the bluffs, the views down to the river and across the valley are indescribable. Between the bluffs the trail drops down and lets hikers get completely taken aback by the beauty of the forest.

Start: Spring Creek/Buffalo River Trailhead off of Spring Creek Road
Distance: 11.6 miles out and back
Hiking time: About 6 to 7 hours
Difficulty: More challenging due to length and elevation changes
Trail surface: Forested path, dirt trail
Best season: Best in early spring and late fall for cooler temperatures
Other trail users: Bikers and equestrians

Canine compatibility: No dogs permitted
Fees and permits: None
Schedule: Open year-round
Maps: USGS Gauge; National Geographic Trails Illustrated Map – Buffalo National River East (#233)
Trail contacts: Buffalo National River, 402 N. Walnut, Suite 136, Harrison, AR 72601; (870) 365-2700; www.nps.gov/buff

Finding the trailhead: From Harriet, Arkansas, drive 3.8 miles north on AR 14 to Spring Creek Road. Turn left (west) onto Spring Creek Road and continue to 5.6 miles and look for the Buffalo River Trail access sign. GPS: N36 03.844' / W93 21.609'

The Hike

There are very few rivers in the United States quite like the Buffalo National River. Established as a national river in 1972, the Buffalo is one of the few remaining undammed rivers in the United States. The river flows for 135 miles through some of the most beautiful scenery that the Ozarks have to offer. The Buffalo River Trail, on the other hand, is still a work in progress. The trail is currently in three sections while several volunteer groups continue to work to connect those trails. Even though the trail is not connected, the three sections that exist are quite breathtaking. Towering bluffs and crystal-clear-river crossings combined with amazing fall foliage and an abundance of spring wildflowers mean the Buffalo River Trail has a little something for everyone. In addition to the Buffalo River Trail are all the other trails that connect to it and lead to places like Hemmed-In Hollow and Big Bluff. The Ozark Highlands Trail and the Old River Trail share several sections with the Buffalo River Trail. The hope one day is that the Buffalo River Trail, Ozark Highlands Trail, and the Ozark Trail in Missouri will all connect to create a network of trails over 1,000 miles long.

Purple coneflower

Locate the Buffalo River Trail Spring Creek access on the north side of the Spring Creek Road and begin hiking northeast. At 1.0 mile you will reach the top of Sitton Eddy Bluff. The views from the bluff are amazing! Continue hiking northwest along the bluff. You will intersect a forest road in another 1.3 miles that comes in from the right (east). This road leads to the east and will take you back to Spring Creek Road, should you need to return there. Over the next couple of miles, the trail drops down a couple hundred feet, then turns north, then east around a few bluffs and up a couple of hollows, and eventually climbs up along Stairstep Bluff.

Begin descending down Stairstep Bluff to eventually cross Kimball Creek at 3.4 miles. For the next 0.8 mile you will be climbing about 480 vertical feet up the next set of bluffs. The trail begins switchbacking up the sandstone bluff to the east. The trail soon turns back to the west, where it will stay level until it reaches the Kimball Bluff overlook at 4.0 miles. From the overlook, climb up about another 80 vertical feet to the top of Kimball Bluff, where the trail will travel along the rim of the bluff for about a mile. The trail begins to switchback down through the woods for about 0.8 mile to a creek. At the creek the trail turns left (northwest) and follows the creek

Buffalo River Trail—Spring Creek Section

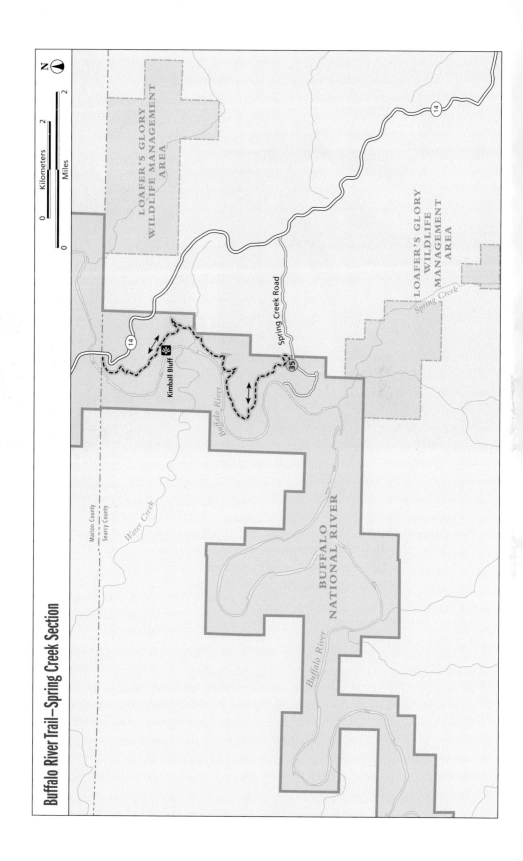

Sensitive Briar

to the river road. Turn right (northeast) onto the road at 5.5 miles and follow it to the Highway 14 Bridge Trailhead and parking lot at 5.8 miles. Turn around and return to the Spring Creek Trailhead at 11.6 miles.

Miles and Directions

- **0.0** Locate the Buffalo River Trail Spring Creek access on the north side of Spring Creek Road and begin hiking northeast.
- **1.0** Reach the top of Sitton Eddy Bluff.
- **1.3** Cross an old forest road that intersects from the right (east).
- **3.4** Cross Kimball Creek.
- **4.0** Arrive at the Kimball Bluff overlook.
- **5.5** The trail joins a forest road. Turn right (east) onto the road.
- **5.8** Reach the Highway 14 Bridge Trailhead. Return to the Spring Creek Trailhead via the same route.
- **11.6** Arrive back at the Spring Creek Trailhead access.

36 Buffalo National River: Indian Rockhouse Trail

There is a great opportunity to see a large variety of birds and other wildlife along this easy trail that traverses a great diversity of landscapes. Along this route that follows the Indian Rockhouse Trail, you will hike hillsides and along creek beds to a bluff shelter once used by Native Americans. Bring your binoculars and look for wild turkeys, white-tailed deer, and woodpeckers along the trail.

Start: Indian Rockhouse Trailhead parking area
Distance: 3.0-mile loop
Hiking time: About 2 hours
Difficulty: Moderate due to a few inclines and length
Trail surface: Forested trail
Best season: Best in early spring and late fall for cooler temperatures, wildflowers, and fall colors
Other trail users: Hikers only
Canine compatibility: No dogs permitted

Fees and permits: None
Schedule: Open year-round
Maps: USGS Cozahome; trail map available at the visitor center
Trail contacts: Park Superintendent, Buffalo National River, 402 N. Walnut St., Suite 136, Harrison, AR 72601; (870) 741-5443; www .nps.gov/buff. Buffalo Point Visitor Center, (870) 449-4311; emergency dispatch (888) 692-1162.

Finding the trailhead: From Yellville, drive south on AR 14 for 14 miles. Turn east on AR 268 and travel 2.5 miles to the Indian Rockhouse Trailhead on the right. GPS: N36 04.890' / W92 34.142'

The Hike

The Buffalo National River offers a wide range of recreational opportunities. The water that flows down the 132-mile river passes through rapids and clear pools, past towering bluffs and densely wooded hillsides. The area is rich with wildlife: Look for elk, deer, turkeys, and even black bears. The Indian Rockhouse Trail showcases some of the best that this exceptional area has to offer. Crystal-clear creeks and springs, lush forests, an amazing bluff shelter, and even an area known as a natural bathtub are just a few of the highlights hikers will experience on the Indian Rockhouse Trail. Older children will really enjoy all there is to offer on this hike.

The hike begins on the north side of AR 268, across from the Indian Rock-house Trailhead parking area. Begin hiking northwest on the obvious trail. You will notice a trail coming in from the left (west), which will be the trail you

Indian Rockhouse Cave ▶

return on. Continue northwest on the trail as it descends through the hardwood woodland. In the evening look for deer, as they can often be seen bedding down near the trail.

At 0.3 mile come to Sinkhole Icebox. The short path that leads to the left (northwest) will take you to a large sinkhole. Sinkholes, springs, caves, and disappearing streams are all common in the Ozarks because of the area's karst topography, which causes the limestone and dolomite rock to dissolve underground. Sinkhole Icebox gets its name because the air within the cavern remains a cool 56°F even at the height of summer. Please stick to the trail when visiting Sinkhole Icebox. A sinkhole is cavity in the ground, caused by erosion, that provides a passageway for groundwater to reach underground caves. Due to erosion, areas surrounding sinkholes may not be stable. Be sure to respect the natural beauty of the area and refrain from throwing rocks or trash into sinkhole. After checking out the sinkhole, continue hiking northeast.

Pass a small waterfall at 0.6 mile and reach the Old Zinc Mine shortly thereafter at 0.7 mile. The abandoned zinc mine is a reminder of the Ozarks' past. Zinc was discovered in the area in the 1880s, and during World War I many landowners turned to prospecting in hopes of getting rich. Few succeeded, and small mines like this were soon abandoned. After viewing the mine continue hiking northeast, following the Panther Creek drainage. This intermittent stream only flows during part of the year.

At 1.2 miles the trail joins an old asphalt service road for a short distance. It soon returns to a gravel path. Follow the signs pointing you toward Indian Rockhouse. The trail forks at 1.5 miles. Stay right (northwest). The trail to the left will be the trail you take to return to the trailhead, but you'll want to visit the Indian Rockhouse first! Continue hiking west, coming to the impressive Indian Rockhouse at 1.7 miles. Once inside, it is not hard to imagine that prehistoric bluff-dwelling Native Americans once used this bluff shelter. While there are no ruins to be seen inside the shelter, take a moment to wander about and ponder what life may have been like here thousands of years ago.

After thoroughly exploring Indian Rockhouse, make your way back to the return trail at 1.9 miles. Turn right (southeast) and cross a small footbridge. After a very short distance, pass by Pebble Springs at 2.0 miles. Come to a fork in the trail at 2.2 miles and stay right (southwest), passing a feature known as the Natural Bathtub. This tub-shaped depression in the stream's bedrock looks so inviting, you'll struggle to resist dipping your toes in on a hot, summer day.

At 2.7 miles come to the rock quarry area. This spot also serves as a reminder of the past as the Civilian Conservation Corp (CCC) used it during the 1930s to mine rock for constructing cabins, pavilions, and other stone structures in the area. Much of the CCC's work is still evident today. At 2.9 miles cross through a gate and turn left (southeast). The trail parallels AR 268 to the trailhead. At 3.0 miles arrive back at the trailhead parking area.

Indian Rockhouse Trail

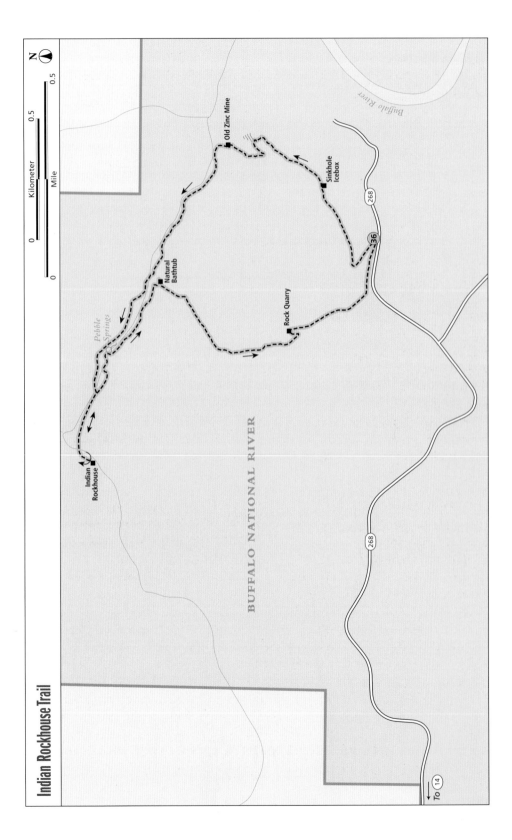

Indian Rockhouse

Pebble Springs

Natural Bathtub

Old Zinc Mine

Sinkhole Icebox

Rock Quarry

BUFFALO NATIONAL RIVER

Buffalo River

268

36

268

To 14

N

Kilometer

Mile

0   0.5   0.5

0   0.5

Miles and Directions

0.0 From the Indian Rockhouse Trailhead parking area, cross AR 268 and hike northwest on the obvious path. After a very short distance, come to the return trail on the left (west).

0.3 Come to the Sinkhole Icebox and continue northeast on the path.

0.6 Pass by a small waterfall and continue north.

0.7 Come to the Old Zinc Mine and continue northwest.

1.2 The trail joins an old asphalt service road for a short distance, then turns to gravel again. Follow the signs for Indian Rockhouse.

1.5 Stay right (northwest) at the fork in the trail. The trail to the left (southeast) is the return trail.

1.7 Reach Indian Rockhouse. Explore the bluff shelter, then retrace your steps back to the return trail.

1.9 Come to the return trail, turn right (southeast), and cross a small footbridge.

2.0 Pass Pebble Springs.

2.2 Stay right (southwest) at the fork in the trail to return to the trailhead. Pass the Natural Bathtub.

2.7 Come to rock quarry. Stay right to return to the trailhead.

2.9 Cross through gates and turn left (southeast) to return to the trailhead.

3.0 Arrive back at the trailhead.

37 Norfork Lake Recreation Area: Robinson Point Trail

This 2.7-mile hike strolls out to a beautiful overlook of one of America's clearest lakes. In fact, the lake is one of the top ten best lakes for activities like scuba diving in the United States. The Robinson Point Trail gives hikers wonderful views and access to the lake. The Robinson Point Overlook makes for great picnicking or just observing all that the area has to offer.

Start: From the Robinson Point Trailhead at the Robinson Point Park entrance

Distance: 2.7-mile lollipop

Hiking time: About 2 hours

Difficulty: Easy

Trail surface: Forested trail

Best season: Best in early spring and late fall for cooler temperatures and wildflowers

Other trail users: Hikers only

Canine compatibility: Leashed dogs permitted

Fees and permits: None

Schedule: Open year-round

Maps: USGS Norfork Dam North; trail map available at park entrance station

Trail contacts: US Army Corps of Engineers, PO Box 867, Little Rock, AR 72203-0867; (501) 324-5551; www.swl.usace.army.mil

Finding the trailhead: From Mountain Home, Arkansas, drive east on US 62 for 7.6 miles. Turn right (south) onto Robinson Point Road and continue to 9.3 miles to the trailhead and parking area on the right (south). GPS: N36 21.423' / W92 14.801'

The Hike

Norfork Lake is surrounded by land that is owned and managed by the US Army Corps of Engineers. The lake itself has over 550 miles of shoreline and over 22,000 surface acres, all of which attract fishermen year-round since there are no seasonal closures on the lake. Mild winters don't usually cause the lake to freeze over either. There are no buildings on the US Army Corps property that surrounds the lake, which helps to preserve the primitive experience sought by many outdoor-recreation enthusiasts. The 25,000 acres of Corps property is under careful watch by wildlife-management programs and is open to the public to give amateur naturalists, birders, and hunters an excellent place to take part in numerous recreational opportunities.

Most people do not come to Norfork Lake as a hiking destination. Instead, they come to get out on the crystal-clear waters and fish for largemouth and smallmouth bass, white bass, crappie, and catfish. Others come just to get out on the water and ski or boat while others come to scuba-dive in the waters of one of America's top ten lakes known for excellent underwater visibility. The lake offers diving depths up to 195 feet and scuba-instruction programs in the area use the lake to their full advantage to bring those crowds in. Just a short drive from Norfork Lake are numerous other outdoor-recreation opportunities including mountain biking on the Pigeon

Robinson Point Trail

Creek National Recreation Trail System and backpacking options in the nearby Ozark National Forest.

Locate the Robinson Point Trailhead and parking area just before you reach the day-use entrance station at the Robinson Point Park. Entering the park requires a fee, but because the trailhead is outside the fee area, you do not need to pay. Begin hiking south on the trail through the piney glades. Reach a trail junction at 0.2 mile. Turn right (southwest) to continue on the main trail; left (southeast) leads to a park road. The trail winds west and then southeast around a lake inlet, then leads away from the shoreline for a bit before returning just before you reach the beginning of the loop portion of the hike at 1.1 miles.

Turn right (southwest) to hike up away from the lake. At 1.3 miles you will arrive at the Robinson Point Overlook. Caution is recommended here, as the bluffs can be steep in some areas. Leave the overlook, hiking northeast back down toward Norfork Lake. The trail is rocky and rugged and circles back around to end the loop portion at 1.6 miles. Turn right (north) to return to the Robinson Point Trailhead and parking area at 2.7 miles.

Robinson Point Trail

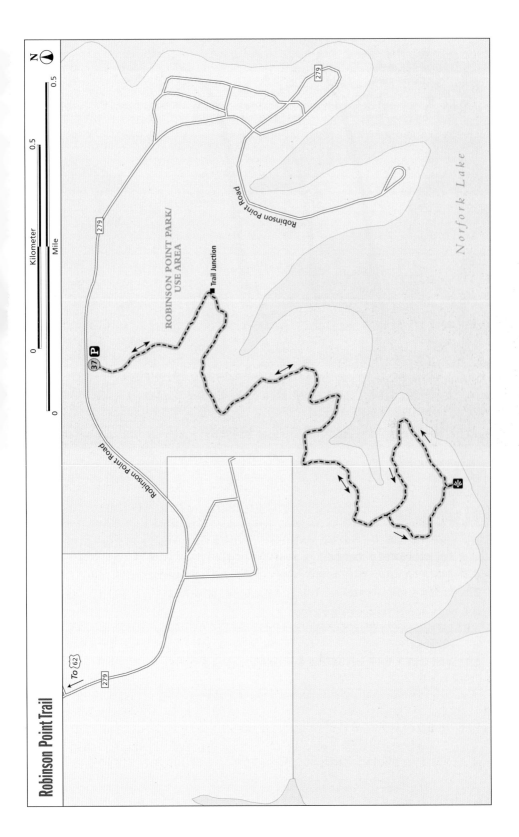

N

0.5   0.5
Kilometer
0   Mile   0.5

To 62

279

Robinson Point Road

279

37 P

ROBINSON POINT PARK/
USE AREA

Trail Junction

Robinson Point Road

279

Norfork Lake

View of Norfork Lake

Miles and Directions

0.0 Locate the Robinson Point Trail just before the entrance to the Robinson Point Park on the right (south) side of the road.

0.2 Turn right (southwest) to continue on the main trail. Left (east) leads to a park road.

1.1 Turn right (southwest) to begin hiking the loop portion of the hike.

1.3 Arrive at the Robinson Point Overlook.

1.6 The loop portion of the hike ends. Turn right (north) to return to the trailhead and parking area.

2.7 Arrive back at the Robinson Point Trailhead and parking area.

Honorable Mentions

F Winthrop P. Rockefeller Boy Scout Trail

This 12.0-mile loop trail is located in Petit Jean State Park. The Boy Scout Trail connects with and follows portions of almost every trail in Petit Jean State Park. Marked with white blazes, the trail highlights the different habitats and visits many of the park's sights, including Rockhouse Cave, waterfalls, historical structures, and towering bluffs. The park requests that hikers register at the visitor center if attempting the entire trail. To reach the trailhead, take exit 108 off I-40 at Morrilton and travel 9 miles south on AR 9. Turn west on AR 154 and travel 12 miles to the park. From Dardanelle, travel 7 miles south on AR 7. Turn east on AR 154 and drive 16 miles to the park. For more information on the Boy Scout Trail or to obtain a trail map, contact Petit Jean State Park, 1285 Petit Jean Mountain Rd., Morrilton, AR 72110; (501) 727-5441; petitjeanstatepark.com; petitjean@arkansas.com.

G Base Trail to East Summit and West Summit Trails

Located in Pinnacle Mountain State Park, this 3.0-mile loop hike combines several of the park's trails to form an interesting day hike. From the boat launch, hike the 1.25-mile Base Trail to its intersection with the East Summit Trail. Hike west on the East Summit Trail to the 1,011-foot summit of Pinnacle Mountain. From the summit, continue west on the West Summit Trail to the picnic area, which is just to the west of the boat launch. Highlights include good views of the Little Maumelle River. The trailhead is located at the West Summit picnic area. To reach the park, take exit 9 off I-430 and travel west on AR 10 for 7 miles. Turn west on AR 300 and drive 2 miles to the park. For more information or to obtain a trail map, contact Pinnacle Mountain State Park, 11901 Pinnacle Valley Rd., Little Rock, AR 72223; (501) 868-5806; www.arkansasstateparks.com/pinnaclemountain; pinnaclemountain@arkansas.com.

H Cecil Cove Loop Trail

The 7.0-mile Cecil Cove Loop Trail combines several trails in the Erbie Trails areas. The hike begins near the historic Erbie Church and begins a gentle descent down an old road, passing several interesting rock formations, caves, an old cemetery, and several historical structures. Tall bluffs offer several good views of the Buffalo River. The trail crosses the Cecil Creek five times in the first few miles of the hike; great caution should be used when crossing the creek, particularly after heavy rainfall. Pets are not permitted on the Cecil Cove Loop Trail. From Harrison, drive south on AR 7 for 17 miles. Turn right (west) onto the Erbie Road and drive 7 miles to the trailhead, located just west of the Erbie Church. For more information, to check road and trail conditions, and to obtain a map of the area, contact Buffalo National River, 402 N.

Walnut St., Suite 136, Harrison, AR 72601 (870-741-5443; www.nps.gov/buff) or the Pruitt Ranger Station at (870) 446-5373.

Hideout Hollow

Located near and managed by the Buffalo National River, the Hideout Hollow Trail is a short but interesting day hike. Once used by a group of World War II draft dodgers know as the Slacker Gang, this easy hike offers good views of the Cecil Cove valley and the surrounding mountains. A 50-foot waterfall and interesting box canyon make for a fun excursion. Pets are not permitted on the Hideout Hollow Trail. From Harrison, drive south on AR 43 for 18.5 miles to Compton. Turn left on the dirt road across from the Compton Post Office and travel 3 miles on that road to the signed trailhead parking area. For more information, to check road and trail conditions, and to obtain a map of the area, contact Buffalo National River, 402 N. Walnut St., Suite 136, Harrison, AR 72601 (870-741-5443; www.nps.gov/buff) or the Pruitt Ranger Station at (870) 446-5373.

Sugar Loaf Mountain Nature Trail

The scenic 1.6-mile Sugar Loaf Mountain Nature Trail, a National Recreation Trail, is an interesting, short day hike that explores Sugar Loaf Mountain Island. Rising 540 feet above Greers Ferry Lake, the island is covered with a pine and hardwood woodland. Highlights of the trail include towering bluffs and intricate rock formations. The summit provides a panoramic view of the surrounding lake and Ozark Mountains. Sugar Loaf Mountain is only accessible by boat, and restroom facilities are not available on the island. Sugar Loaf Mountain Island is located on the western end of the upper lake. The nearest marina is Sugar Loaf Use Area. From Heber Springs, drive west on AR 25/AR 5/Heber Springs Road and continue on AR 25 South to AR 16/Edgemont Road. Turn right (west) on AR 16/Edgemont Road and drive 12 miles. Turn left (west) onto AR 92 West and proceed 1.3 miles. Take a slight right onto AR 337 North for 1.3 miles to County Road 623/Resort Road, which leads to the marina. For more information, contact Greers Ferry Project Office, 700 Heber Springs Rd. N., Heber Springs, AR 72543; (501) 362-2416; www.swl.usace.army.mil; ceswl-gf@usace.army.mil.

Oklahoma Region

The western edge of the Ozarks reaches across the southeast tip of Kansas and the northeast corner of Oklahoma. The Oklahoma region of the Ozarks Plateau is known more for its numerous lakes and fishing opportunities than it is for its hiking, but there are a few good trails to be hiked here. Home to the Cherokee Nation, this part of the Ozark Mountains offers hikers similar terrain to that found in northern Arkansas and southern Missouri. Wooded, rolling hills can be found throughout this region and provide spectacular spring and fall viewing for hikers. Many of the state parks in Oklahoma offer resort-style accommodations for its visitors and offer numerous recreational opportunities.

The Ozarks offer remarkable biodiversity in the United States. The region's karst caves and sinkholes have been carved out over thousands of years and have created amazing cave environments that support a very diverse animal community. Over 200 species are restricted to the area, and around 160 of those species can be found nowhere else on earth. Some of the endangered species in the area include the Ozark big-eared bat, the gray bat, the Indiana bat, and the Ozark cavefish. Over one hundred species of fish live in the Ozarks, and this part of Oklahoma proudly boasts some of the best fly-fishing in the area.

38 Greenleaf State Park: Greenleaf Lake Hiking Trail

This spectacular hike traverses the hills on the east side of Greenleaf Lake and the state park. Hikers have the opportunity to explore the rolling terrain of the park on this 12.8-mile trail, which has become known as the Ankle Express Trail. The hiking/backpacking trail is a collaborative effort of three local organizations: Camp Gruber, Greenleaf State Park, and the Oklahoma Ankle Express Hiking Club.

Start: From the trailhead for the Greenleaf Lake Hiking Trail in Greenleaf State Park
Distance: 12.8-mile lollipop
Hiking time: About 6 to 8 hours
Difficulty: More challenging due to length
Trail surface: Forested trail, dirt path, and a highway crossing
Best season: Late fall, winter, and spring to avoid the heat and insects

Other trail users: Mountain bikers
Canine compatibility: Leashed dogs permitted
Fees and permits: None
Schedule: Open year-round
Maps: USGS Webbers Falls; trail map available at the visitor center
Trail contacts: Greenleaf State Park, Route 1, Box 119, Braggs, OK 74423; (918) 487-5622; www.travelok.com/listings/view.profile/id.3236

Finding the trailhead: From Gore, Oklahoma, drive 8.5 miles northwest on OK 10. Turn right (east) into Greenleaf State Park and follow the park road past the visitor center at 9.2 miles, then stay right toward the trailhead at 9.4 miles. Arrive at the trailhead on the right (south) at 9.6 miles. GPS: N35 37.45' / W95 10.216'

The Hike

The Oklahoma region of the Ozarks is not nearly as well known for its hiking trails as the Missouri and Arkansas regions. This section of the Ozarks is known for its numerous lakes and great fishing opportunities, and Greenleaf State Park is no different. The park is one of Oklahoma's original seven state parks and is known to Oklahomans as a very family-friendly park with ample facilities, including 1930s Civilian Conservation Corp–built cabins, tent camping, RV camping, showers, picnic areas, shelters, laundry facilities, and much more. Many people come to Greenleaf State Park to camp and fish and just enjoy nature. The handful of people who do hike usually make their way to the highlight of the Greenleaf Lake Hiking Trail, the swinging bridge. The bridge spans over a small inlet, and the hike to the swinging bridge and back is 5.2 miles, a good hike all by itself. However, the best scenery actually takes place after the bridge. The Greenleaf Lake Hiking Trail travels along Greenleaf Lake and then climbs up the hillside to offer better views of the lake and the surrounding area, especially in the early spring and late fall when the trees are not so full.

Swinging bridge on Greenleaf Lake Hiking Trail ▶

Greenleaf Lake Hiking Trail

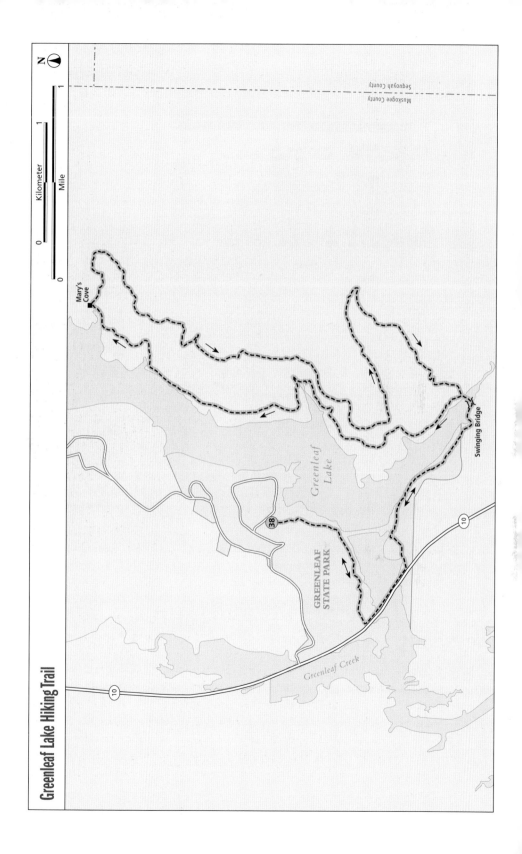

Greenleaf Lake Hiking Trail

Leave the Greenleaf Lake Hiking Trailhead and kiosk by hiking south into the woods on the dirt path. The trail travels along the edge of the woods for the first part, and you will pass some campsites, a shower facility, and eventually a large ADA-accessible cabin that is available to rent. After the cabin the trail slowly turns west and then crosses a paved access road at 0.7 mile. The road is used by fishermen for access to Greenleaf Lake. Just a short distance after crossing the access road and reentering the woods, you will come to OK 10 at 1.0 mile. Turn left (southeast) to cross the bridge over Greenleaf Lake, being very careful as motorists tend to be quite careless sometimes. Reach the end of the bridge at 1.3 miles and turn left (east) back on the trail and into the woods. At 1.5 miles cross another lake access road, which is no

longer maintained and not used very much, and continue hiking east. From here, the trail travels up high on the hillside above the lake. Keep an eye out for wildlife—deer and turkeys are commonly seen along the trail.

At 2.6 miles arrive at the swinging bridge. The trail is well traveled up to this point and can be a little tougher to navigate during the summer months from here on with all the overgrowth. Watch for the blue blazes on the trees in these overgrown areas and you should be fine. Cross the swinging bridge and turn left (northwest) onto the loop portion of the hike. To the right (northeast) is your return trail. Hike along as several views of Greenleaf Lake are offered below and the trail joins an old forest road at 3.0 miles and then quickly bears right (northeast) back onto singletrack trail into the woods. At 3.9 miles the trail crosses an inlet and then makes a sharp left (northwest) turn. Watch for the blue blazes here for help. The trail continues along the lake for the next bit until you reach Mary's Cove at 5.6 miles. Mary's Cove tends to be a popular place for extended breaks, lunches, and overnight camping.

From Mary's Cove, turn right (east) onto the white-blazed connector trail that climbs up the rocky and rugged section of trail. At 6.0 miles reach the end of the connector trail and turn right (south) back onto the blue-blazed trail. Hike along as the trail climbs higher up onto the ridge and you eventually come to an open glade area at 9.8 miles that is full of wildflowers in the spring. Just after the glade the trail begins descending down a rocky slope and meets back up with the swinging bridge at 10.2 miles. Turn left (southwest) to cross the bridge again and return to the Greenleaf Lake Hiking Trailhead and parking area at 12.8 miles.

Miles and Directions

0.0 Leave the Greenleaf Lake Hiking Trailhead by hiking south into the forest.

0.7 The trail crosses a paved access road.

1.0 The trail leaves the woods and turns left (southeast) to cross over a bridge along OK 10.

1.3 Reach the other side of the bridge and turn left (east) back into the forest on the hiking trail.

1.5 The trail crosses over an old lake access road that is no longer maintained and not often used by fishermen.

2.6 Come to and cross the swinging bridge that crosses over a small inlet of Greenleaf Lake.

3.0 The trail connects briefly with an old forest road and then bears right (northeast) back onto the singletrack trail.

3.9 The trail crosses over an inlet and then makes a sharp left (northwest).

5.6 Reach Mary's Cove and locate the white-blazed connector. Turn right (east) onto the connector trail.

6.0 Turn right (south) back onto the blue-blazed section of the hiking trail.

9.8 The trail crosses through an open glade and then begins descending down the hillside.

10.2 Return to the swinging bridge. Turn left (southwest) to cross the bridge and return to the trailhead.

12.8 Arrive back at the Greenleaf Lake Hiking Trailhead and parking area.

Honorable Mentions

K McGee Creek National Scenic Recreation Area Trail System

Located just north of McGee Creek State Park in Atoka, the 8,900-acre McGee Creek Natural Scenic Recreation Area Trail System hosts over 20 miles of hiking trails. While hiking, mountain biking, and horseback riding are acceptable on all trails, no motorized vehicles are allowed on any of the trails. Before hiking any of the trails, you must register for a permit from the Natural Scenic Recreation Area office. Permits are free and help keep track of the number people using the trails. From Atoka, travel east on OK 3 East. Turn left (north) onto South Centerpoint Road and drive 8.4 miles. Continue on Schoellkopf Lane for 2.5 miles. For more information, contact McGee Creek State Park, 576-A S. McGee Creek Lake Rd., Atoka, OK 74525; (580) 889-5822.

Illinois Region

While not considered a part of the true Ozark Plateau, the Shawnee Hills of southwestern Illinois are commonly referred to as the Illinois Ozarks. The rough, unglaciated area is so similar in both topography and beauty to the Ozarks that we just had to include a sampling of trails in this area. Like much of the Ozarks, towering bluffs, interesting rock formations, and diverse flora and fauna make hiking here a pleasure. The two trails featured here are located within the Shawnee National Forest. Trails are accessible almost year-round and each season offers unique beauty. Dogwoods, redbuds, and wildflowers put on quite a display in springtime. Lush forests provide good shade in summer. Red, orange, and gold leaves make fall a beautiful time to visit. And even winter can be quite fascinating, with giant icicles hanging off the bluffs, caves, and rock formations.

The Shawnee Hills and Shawnee National Forest are one of the most extensively forested regions in the state. The hills and forest are home to many rare and endangered plants and animals. Copperheads, timber rattlesnakes, and green water snakes all live in this region and can be viewed during a popular time of year when the snakes migrate across an area known as "Snake Road." (Google it for details.) In all, the rugged Illinois region of the Ozarks is home to over five hundred wildlife species that take refuge in dominant oak and hickory forests.

39 Shawnee National Forest: Little Grand Canyon Trail

This dynamic loop hike traverses a variety of terrains in a very short distance, making it one of the best and most highly recommended short day hikes in this collection of trails. Located in the Shawnee National Forest, this trail features exposed bluffs, an erosion-carved canyon, a seasonal waterfall, and several rock overhangs, making it one of the most interesting areas in the entire region.

Start: From the Little Grand Canyon Trailhead in the Shawnee National Forest
Distance: 3.0-mile loop
Hiking time: About 2 hours
Difficulty: More challenging due to steep climbs and slippery rocks
Trail surface: Forested trail, rock
Best season: Fall through spring
Other trail users: Hikers only
Canine compatibility: Leashed dogs permitted
Fees and permits: None
Schedule: Open year-round
Maps: USGS Gorham
Trail contacts: Shawnee National Forest, 50 Highway 145 S., Harrisburg, IL 62946; (618) 253-7114; www.fs.usda.gov

Finding the trailhead: From Carbondale, Illinois, drive 4.6 miles west on Old Highway 13 and then turn left onto IL 127 South. Continue 2.9 miles on IL 127 South before turning right onto Orchard Hill Road. Drive 2.7 miles on Orchard Hill Road and take a slight right onto Poplar Ridge Road. After 1.2 miles stay straight on Hickory Ridge Road. Drive 2.4 miles on Hickory Ridge Road and then turn right onto Little Grand Canyon Road. Follow Little Grand Canyon Road until it dead-ends in the parking area. The trailhead is located at the southwest corner of the parking area. GPS: N37 40.842' / W89 23.719'

The Hike

The Little Grand Canyon National Natural Landmark is a small but dramatic part of the 280,000-acre Shawnee National Forest. Located in Jackson County, Illinois, the deep box canyon has been slowly eroding over time and now boasts exposed, majestic bluffs.

Visitors to the Little Grand Canyon area will witness typical southern Illinois landscapes. Rich oak and hickory forests tower above sycamore and beech trees. Just south of Little Grand Canyon is a place known as Snake Road. Each year the road is closed down to accommodate several species of snakes, including timber rattlesnakes, western cottonmouths, and the endangered green water snake, as they migrate to and from their winter hibernation spots, which include the Little Grand Canyon.

The Little Grand Canyon Trail is a 3.0-mile hike that begins with a roller coaster–like ridge descent to a scenic overlook. Hikers can stop, enjoy the view, and return to the parking lot, or continue into the canyon below.

View from Little Grand Canyon Trail

The trailhead is located at the southwest corner of the parking area, just to the right (west) of the outhouses. Begin hiking southwest on the obvious, gravel and dirt trail. Follow the trail as it traverses Viney Ridge through a thick forest of maple, oak, sassafras, beech, and tulip trees. Pass several wooden benches before reaching a large scenic overlook on Chalk Bluff at 1.2 miles. Here you have a good view of the Big Muddy River to the west. At this point the trail curves to the right (southeast) and gradually begins to descend the ridge.

At 1.4 miles the trail grows noticeably steeper and you enter the moss-covered sandstone canyon. Carefully descend, alternating between following the trail and the natural drainage. Look closely and you will notice that steps have been etched into the rock in several areas, a work project completed by the Civilian Conservation Corps in the 1930s.

At 1.8 miles reach the bottom of the canyon and begin following the trail, now marked with white diamonds, to the east. Cross a small creek at 2.1 miles and

Little Grand Canyon Trail

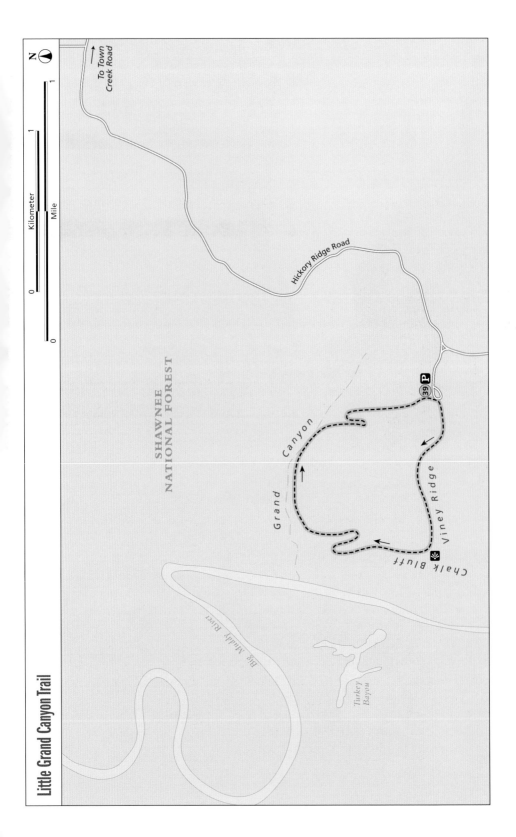

continue east, passing tall bluffs. At 2.4 miles the trail curves to the right (south) and into another slippery sandstone drainage. Follow the drainage, again using caution and looking for steps as you pass over several small, seasonal waterfalls. At the top of the drainage, turn left (east) and ascend the moderately steep trail back to the parking area.

Miles and Directions

0.0 Begin hiking southwest along Viney Ridge.

1.2 Come to the scenic overlook at Chalk Bluff.

1.4 Descend the slippery sandstone canyon.

1.8 Reach the bottom of the canyon and begin hiking east.

2.1 Cross a small creek and continue hiking east.

2.4 Come to the second sandstone canyon and carefully ascend, hiking south. At the top of the canyon, turn left (east) onto the obvious dirt trail.

3.0 Arrive back at the parking area and trailhead.

Little Grand Canyon passage to trailhead

40 Shawnee National Forest: Panther Den Trail

This easy day hike introduces you to the forests within the Shawnee National Forest, located in the Ozark and Shawnee Hills of southern Illinois. The Panther Den Trail provides easy access to one of the most interesting rock formations in the area. A short hike allows for hours of exploration.

Start: From the Panther Den Trail parking area in the Shawnee National Forest
Distance: 2.0 miles out and back
Hiking time: About 1 hour for the hike; allow more time to explore the rock formations
Difficulty: Easy due to length and relatively flat terrain
Trail surface: Forested trail
Best season: Any

Other trail users: Equestrians
Canine compatibility: Leashed dogs permitted
Fees and permits: None
Schedule: Open year-round
Maps: USGS Lick Creek
Trail contacts: Shawnee National Forest, 50 Highway 145 S., Harrisburg, IL 62946; (618) 253-7114; www.fs.usda.gov

Finding the trailhead: From Carbondale, Illinois, take Giant City Road for 7 miles to Grassy Road. Turn left onto Grassy Road and drive 3 miles before turning right onto Rocky Comfort Road. Follow Rocky Comfort Road (staying right at 1.9 miles at the Y) for 4.1 miles to Panther Den Road. Turn left and drive 1.5 miles to Panther Den Lane. Turn left again and drive 0.6 mile down the gravel road to the parking area and trailhead on the right. GPS: N37 34.782' / W89 5.295'

The Hike

In 1990 the US Congress designated southern Illinois's Panther Den as a wilderness area. Panther Den Wilderness Area totals 1,195 acres, 1,081 acres of which is managed by the Shawnee National Forest, with the Crab Orchard National Wildlife Refuge managing the remaining acreage.

The 160-mile River-to-River Trail runs through Panther Den Wilderness Area and is the trail that receives the most recognition. However, the several trails that support and branch off of the River-to-River Trail offer some amazing opportunities. Hikers choosing the Panther Den Trail are in for a treat as they will soon come into an area believed to have once been a large waterway that over time has created a "hiker's playground."

The Panther Den Trail is a quick 2.0-mile out-and-back hike that leaves plenty of time to explore a remarkable maze of 70-foot-high cliffs in which huge blocks have split off from one another to create a network of crevices, passageways, and cave-like "rooms."

Giant rocks at Panther Den ▶

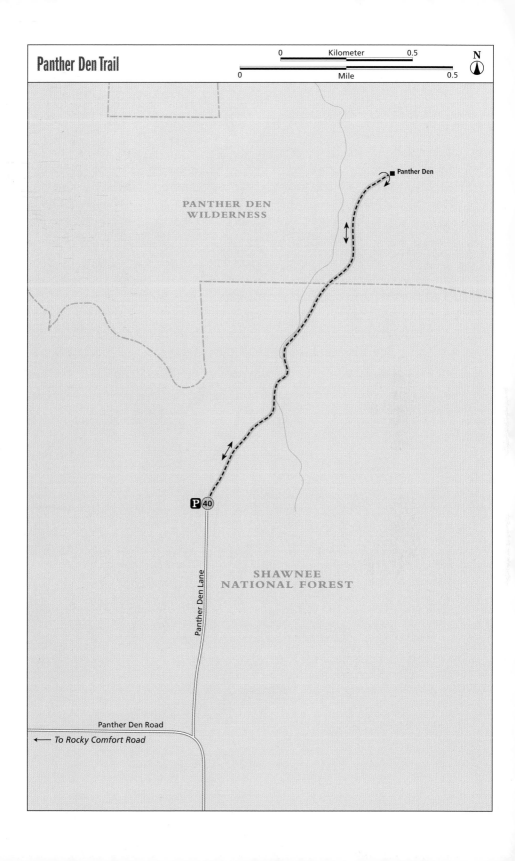

Panther Den Trail

0   Kilometer   0.5

0   Mile   0.5

N

Panther Den

PANTHER DEN
WILDERNESS

P 40

Panther Den Lane

SHAWNEE
NATIONAL FOREST

Panther Den Road

← To Rocky Comfort Road

From the parking area, locate the information kiosk and trailhead. Begin hiking northeast on the obvious dirt trail, which is marked with white diamonds. At 0.3 mile a trail branches to the right—avoid this trail and continue on Panther Den Trail (Forest Service Trail 371). Soon after this you will pass a fire ring/camping area on the left (west).

At 0.4 mile cross the creek and continue hiking northeast. At 0.7 mile cross the creek again and enter Panther Den Wilderness Area. Just after entering the wilderness area, come to a fork in the trail and bear left (northeast). After 1 mile reach the Panther Den and explore the several paths that lead through the labyrinth of rocks and cliffs. When you are through exploring, return to the trailhead via the same route.

Miles and Directions

- **0.0**　From the trailhead, hike northeast on the obvious dirt trail.
- **0.3**　Avoid the trail that forks to the right and continue hiking northeast.
- **0.4**　Cross a creek and continue hiking northeast.
- **0.7**　Enter Panther Den Wilderness Area and bear left (northeast) at the fork in the trail.
- **1.0**　Reach Panther Den. After exploring this area return to the trailhead via the same route.
- **2.0**　Arrive at the parking area.

Honorable Mentions

L Piney Creek Ravine Trail

Featuring the largest concentration of prehistoric rock art in Illinois and several rare plant species, the 2.5-mile Piney Creek Trail offers visitors a pleasant day hike rich in both natural and cultural history. Believed to date back to the Late Woodland (AD 500–1000) and Mississippian (AD 1000–1550) eras, the petroglyphs and pictographs are unlike any others in the Ozarks. Much of the "graffiti" is even old, dating back to early settlers of the region (unfortunately, some of the graffiti is more recent, and any signs of vandalism should be reported to the Illinois Department of Natural Resources).

Piney Creek Ravine is one of only two places in Illinois where shortleaf pines grow naturally. The ravine forms a moist, sheltered habitat for mosses and liverworts to grow but also offers dry, exposed bluffs perfect for post and blackjack oaks. Hikers coming to Piney Creek Ravine may encounter opossums, cottontails, chipmunks, white-tailed deer, fence lizards, rough green snakes, and copperhead snakes. Timber rattlesnakes have never been reported but are a possibility in the area. From Chester, Illinois, drive south on IL 3 South. South of Chester there is a large brown sign for Piney Creek Ravine directing you to turn left onto Hog Hill Road/CR 20. Follow Hog Hill Road for 3.8 miles to the intersection with Degognia Road. Turn right (east), then immediately left (north), staying on CR 20, which is now Rock Crusher Road. Continue on CR 20/Rock Crusher Road for 1.1 miles to Piney Creek Road. Turn left (west) onto Piney Creek Road and drive 1.6 miles to the large, gravel parking area on the right (east). For more information, contact Piney Creek Ravine, 4301 S. Lake Dr., Chester, IL 62233; (618) 826-2706; http://dnr.state.il.us; dnr.randolph county@illinois.gov.

M Giant City Nature Trail

Giant City State Park has several nice trails that are perfect for family day hikes. The Giant City Nature Trail is a 1.1-mile loop trail that is beautiful year-round. In the spring hundreds of species of wildflowers grow on and around the massive sandstone structures. In the summer the towering tree canopy provides hikers and wildlife with a reprise from the sun. In the fall hikers are treated to a wash of fall color from more than seventy-five species of trees. And in the winter, icicles hang delicately from the overhanging cliffs. Highlights of the trail are the "Giant City Streets," huge sandstone bluffs that jut up on both sides of the trail. From Carbondale, Illinois, drive south on Giant City Road for 10.7 miles and turn right onto Giant City Lodge Road. Drive 0.5 mile and turn left onto Stone Fort Road. Continue 0.4 mile on Stone Fort Road to the Shelter #2 parking area on the right. For more information, contact Giant City State Park, 235 Giant City Rd., Makanda, IL 62958; (618) 457-4836; http://dnr.state.il.us.

The Art of Hiking

When standing nose to nose with a mountain lion, you're probably not too concerned with the issue of ethical behavior in the wild. No doubt you're just terrified. But let's be honest. How often are you nose to nose with a mountain lion? For most of us, a hike into the "wild" means loading up the SUV with expensive gear and driving to a toileted trailhead. Sure, you can mourn how civilized we've become—how GPS units have replaced natural instinct and Gore-Tex stands in for true grit—but the silly gadgets of civilization aside, we have plenty of reason to take pride in how we've matured. With survival now on the back burner, we've begun to understand that we have a responsibility to protect, no longer just conquer, our wild places: that they, not we, are at risk. So please, do what you can. The following section will help you understand better what it means to "do what you can" while still making the most of your hiking experience. Anyone can take a hike, but hiking safely and well is an art requiring preparation and proper equipment.

Trail Etiquette

Leave no trace. Always leave an area just like you found it—if not better than you found it. Avoid camping in fragile, alpine meadows and along the banks of streams and lakes. Use a camp stove versus building a wood fire. Pack up all of your trash and extra food. Bury human waste at least 100 feet from water sources under 6 to 8 inches of topsoil. Don't bathe with soap in a lake, stream, or river—use prepackaged moistened towels to wipe sweat and dirt, or bathe in the water without soap.

Stay on the trail. It's true, a path anywhere leads nowhere new, but purists will just have to get over it. Paths serve an important purpose: They limit impact on natural areas. Straying from a designated trail may seem innocent but it can cause damage to sensitive areas—damage that may take years to recover, if it can recover at all. Even simple shortcuts can be destructive. So please, stay on the trail.

Leave no weeds. Noxious weeds tend to overtake other plants, which in turn affects animals and birds that depend on them for food. To minimize the spread of noxious weeds, hikers should regularly clean their boots, tents, packs, and hiking poles of mud and seeds. Also brush your dog to remove any weed seeds before heading out into a new area.

Keep your dog under control. You can buy a flexi-lead that allows your dog to go exploring along the trail, while allowing you the ability to reel him in should another hiker approach or should he decide to chase a rabbit. Always obey leash laws and be sure to bury your dog's waste or pack it in resealable plastic bags.

Respect other trail users. Often you're not the only one on the trail. With the rise in popularity of multiuse trails, you'll have to learn a new kind of respect, beyond

the nod and "hello" approach you may be used to. First investigate whether you're on a multiuse trail, and assume the appropriate precautions. When you encounter motorized vehicles (ATVs, motorcycles, and 4WDs), be alert. Though they should always yield to the hiker, often they're going too fast or are too lost in the buzz of their engine to react to your presence. If you hear activity ahead, step off the trail just to be safe. Note that you're not likely to hear a mountain biker coming, so be prepared and know ahead of time whether you share the trail with them. Cyclists should always yield to hikers, but that's little comfort to the hiker. Be aware.

When you approach horses or pack animals on the trail, always step quietly off the trail, preferably on the downhill side, and let them pass. If you're wearing a large backpack, it's often a good idea to remove your pack and speak calmly to an animal that seems afraid. To some animals, a hiker wearing a large backpack might appear threatening. Many national forests allow domesticated grazing, usually for sheep and cattle. Make sure your dog doesn't harass these animals, and respect ranchers' rights while you're enjoying yours.

Getting In Shape

Unless you want to be sore—and possibly have to shorten your trip or vacation—be sure to get in shape before a big hike. If you're terribly out of shape, start a walking program early, preferably eight weeks in advance. Start with a 15-minute walk during your lunch hour or after work and gradually increase your walking time to an hour. You should also increase your elevation gain. Walking briskly up hills really strengthens your leg muscles and gets your heart rate up. If you work in a storied office building, take the stairs instead of the elevator. If you prefer going to a gym, walk the treadmill or use a stair machine. You can further increase your strength and endurance by walking with a loaded backpack. Stationary exercises you might consider are squats, leg lifts, sit-ups, and push-ups. Other good ways to get in shape include biking, running, aerobics, and, of course, short hikes. Stretching before and after a hike keeps muscles flexible and helps avoid injuries.

Preparedness

It's been said that failing to plan means planning to fail. So do take the necessary time to plan your trip. Whether going on a short day hike or an extended backpack trip, always prepare for the worst. Simply remembering to pack a copy of the *U.S. Army Survival Manual* is not preparedness. Although it's not a bad idea if you plan on entering truly wild places, it's merely the tourniquet answer to a problem. You need to do your best to prevent the problem from arising in the first place. In order to survive—and to stay reasonably comfortable—you need to concern yourself with the basics: water, food, and shelter. Don't go on a hike without having these bases covered. And don't go on a hike expecting to find these items in the woods.

Small shut-ins along Ozark Trail near Klepzig Mill ▷

Water. Even in frigid conditions, you need at least two quarts of water a day to function efficiently. Add heat and taxing terrain and you can bump that figure up to one gallon. That's simply a base to work from—your metabolism and your level of conditioning can raise or lower that amount. Unless you know your level, assume that you need one gallon of water a day.

Now, where do you plan on getting the water? Preferably not from natural water sources. These sources can be loaded with intestinal disturbers, such as bacteria, viruses, and fertilizers. Giardia, the most common of these disturbers, is a protozoan parasite that lives part of its life cycle as a cyst in water sources. The parasite spreads when mammals defecate in water sources. Once ingested, giardia can induce cramping, diarrhea, vomiting, and fatigue within two days to two weeks after ingestion. Giardiasis is treatable with prescription drugs. If you believe you've contracted giardiasis, see a doctor immediately.

Treating water. The best and easiest solution to avoid polluted water is to carry your water with you. Yet, depending on the nature of your hike and the duration, this may not be an option—one gallon of water weighs eight and a half pounds. In that case you'll need to look into treating water. Regardless of which method you choose, you should always carry some water with you in case of an emergency. Save this reserve until you absolutely need it.

There are three methods of treating water: boiling, chemical treatment, and filtering. If you boil water, it's recommended that you do so for 10 to 15 minutes. This is often impractical because you're forced to exhaust a great deal of your fuel supply. You can opt for chemical treatment, which will kill giardia but will not take care of other chemical pollutants. Another drawback to chemical treatments is the unpleasant taste of the water after it's treated. You can remedy this by adding powdered drink mix to the water. Filters are the preferred method for treating water. Many filters remove giardia, organic and inorganic contaminants, and don't leave an aftertaste. Water filters are far from perfect as they can easily become clogged or leak if a gasket wears out. It's always a good idea to carry a backup supply of chemical treatment tablets in case your filter decides to quit on you.

Food. If we're talking about survival, you can go days without food, as long as you have water. But we're also talking about comfort. Try to avoid foods that are high in sugar and fat like candy bars and potato chips. These food types are harder to digest and are low in nutritional value. Instead, bring along foods that are easy to pack, nutritious, and high in energy (e.g., bagels, nutrition bars, dehydrated fruit, gorp, and jerky). If you are on an overnight trip, easy-to-fix dinners include rice mixes with dehydrated potatoes, corn, pasta with cheese sauce, and soup mixes.

For a tasty breakfast, you can fix hot oatmeal with brown sugar and reconstituted milk powder topped off with banana chips. If you like a hot drink in the morning, bring along herbal tea bags or hot chocolate. If you are a coffee junkie, you can purchase coffee that is packaged like tea bags. You can prepackage all of your meals in

heavy-duty resealable plastic bags to keep food from spilling in your pack. These bags can be reused to pack out trash.

Shelter. The type of shelter you choose depends less on the conditions than on your tolerance for discomfort. Shelter comes in many forms—tent, tarp, lean-to, bivy sack, cabin, cave, etc. If you're camping in the desert, a bivy sack may suffice, but if you're above the tree line and a storm is approaching, a better choice is a three- or four-season tent. Tents are the logical and most popular choice for most backpackers as they're lightweight and packable—and you can rest assured that you always have shelter from the elements. Before you leave on your trip, anticipate what the weather and terrain will be like and plan for the type of shelter that will work best for your comfort level (see "Equipment" later in this section).

Finding a campsite. If there are established campsites, stick to those. If not, start looking for a campsite early—around 3:30 or 4 p.m. Stop at the first decent site you see. Depending on the area, it could be a long time before you find another suitable location. Pitch your camp in an area that's level. Make sure the area is at least 200 feet from fragile areas like lakeshores, meadows, and stream banks. And try to avoid areas thick in underbrush, as they can harbor insects and provide cover for approaching animals.

If you are camping in stormy, rainy weather, look for a rock outcrop or a shelter in the trees to keep the wind from blowing your tent all night. Be sure that you don't camp under trees with dead limbs that might break off on top of you. Also, try to find an area that has an absorbent surface, such as sandy soil or forest duff. This, in addition to camping on a surface with a slight angle, will provide better drainage. By all means, don't dig trenches to provide drainage around your tent—remember, you're practicing zero-impact camping.

If you're in bear country, steer clear of creekbeds or animal paths. If you see any signs of a bear's presence (i.e., scat, footprints), relocate. You'll need to find a campsite near a tall tree where you can hang your food and other items that may attract bears such as deodorant, toothpaste, and soap. Carry a lightweight nylon rope with which to hang your food. As a rule, you should hang your food at least 20 feet from the ground and 5 feet away from the tree trunk. You can put food and other items in a waterproof stuff sack and tie one end of the rope to the stuff sack. To get the other end of the rope over the tree branch, tie a good-size rock to it, and gently toss the rock over the tree branch. Pull the stuff sack up until it reaches the top of the branch and tie it securely. Don't hang your food near your tent! If possible, hang your food at least 100 feet away from your campsite. Alternatives to hanging your food are bear-proof plastic tubes and metal bear boxes.

Lastly, think of comfort. Lie down on the ground where you intend to sleep and see if it's a good fit. For morning warmth (and a nice view to wake up to), have your tent face east.

I know you're tough, but get 10 miles into the woods and develop a blister and you'll wish you had carried that first-aid kit. Face it, it's just plain good sense. Many companies produce lightweight, compact first-aid kits.

Here are a few tips for dealing with and hopefully preventing certain ailments.

Sunburn. Take along sunscreen or sunblock, protective clothing, and a wide-brimmed hat. If you do get a sunburn, treat the area with aloe vera gel, and protect the area from further sun exposure. At higher elevations the sun's radiation can be particularly damaging to skin. Remember that your eyes are vulnerable to this radiation as well. Sunglasses can be a good way to prevent headaches and permanent eye damage from the sun, especially in places where light-colored rock or patches of snow reflect light up in your face.

Blisters. Be prepared to take care of these hike-spoilers by carrying moleskin (a lightly padded adhesive), gauze and tape, or adhesive bandages. An effective way to apply moleskin is to cut out a circle of moleskin and remove the center—like a doughnut—and place it over the blistered area. Cutting the center out will reduce the pressure applied to the sensitive skin. Other products can help you combat blisters. Some are applied to suspicious hot spots before a blister forms to help decrease friction to that area, while others are applied to the blister after it has popped to help prevent further irritation.

Insect bites and stings. You can treat most insect bites and stings by applying hydrocortisone 1 percent cream topically and taking a pain medication such as ibuprofen or acetaminophen to reduce swelling. If you forgot to pack these items, a cold compress or a paste of mud and ashes can sometimes assuage the itching and discomfort. Remove any stingers by using tweezers or scraping the area with your fingernail or a knife blade. Don't pinch the area as you'll only spread the venom.

Some hikers are highly sensitive to bites and stings and may have a serious allergic reaction that can be life threatening. Symptoms of a serious allergic reaction can include wheezing, an asthmatic attack, and shock. The treatment for this severe type of reaction is epinephrine. If you know that you are sensitive to bites and stings, carry a prepackaged kit of epinephrine, which can be obtained only by prescription from your doctor.

Ticks. Ticks can carry diseases such as Rocky Mountain spotted fever and Lyme disease. The best defense is, of course, prevention. If you know you're going to be hiking through an area littered with ticks, wear long pants and a long-sleeved shirt. You can apply a permethrin repellent to your clothing and a deet repellent to exposed skin. At the end of your hike, do a spot-check for ticks (and insects in general). If you do find a tick, grab the head of the tick firmly—with a pair of tweezers if you have them—and gently pull it away from the skin with a twisting motion. Sometimes the mouth parts linger, embedded in your skin. If this happens, try to remove them with a disinfected needle. Clean the affected area with an antibacterial cleanser and then

Cedar Falls

apply triple antibiotic ointment. Monitor the area for a few days. If irritation persists or a white spot develops, see a doctor for possible infection.

Poison ivy, oak, and sumac. These skin irritants can be found most anywhere in North America and come in the form of a bush or a vine, having leaflets in groups of three, five, seven, or nine. Learn how to spot the plants. The oil they secrete can cause an allergic reaction in the form of blisters, usually about 12 hours after exposure. The itchy rash can last from ten days to several weeks. The best defense against these irritants is to wear clothing that covers the arms, legs, and torso. For summer, zip-off cargo pants come in handy. There are also nonprescription lotions you can apply to exposed skin that guard against the effects of poison ivy/oak/sumac and can be washed off with soap and water. If you think you were in contact with the plants, after hiking (or even on the trail during longer hikes) wash with soap and water. Taking a hot shower with soap after you return home from your hike will also help to remove any lingering oil from your skin. Should you contract a rash from any of these plants, use an antihistamine to reduce the itching. If the rash is localized, create

a light bleach/water wash to dry up the area. If the rash has spread, either tough it out or see your doctor about getting a dose of cortisone (available both orally and by injection).

Snakebites. Snakebites are rare in North America. Unless startled or provoked, the majority of snakes will not bite. If you are wise to their habitats and keep a careful eye on the trail, you should be just fine. When stepping over logs, first step on the log, making sure you can see what's on the other side before stepping down. Though your chances of being struck are slim, it's wise to know what to do in the event you are.

If a nonpoisonous snake bites you, allow the wound to bleed a small amount and then cleanse the wounded area with a Betadine solution (10 percent povidone iodine). Rinse the wound with clean water (preferably) or fresh urine (it might sound ugly, but it's sterile). Once the area is clean, cover it with triple antibiotic ointment and a clean bandage. Remember, most residual damage from snakebites, poisonous or otherwise, comes from infection, not the snake's venom. Keep the area as clean as possible and get medical attention immediately.

If somebody in your party is bitten by a poisonous snake, follow these steps:

1. Calm the patient.

2. Remove jewelry, watches, and restrictive clothing, and immobilize the affected limb. Do not elevate the injury. Medical opinions vary on whether the area should be lower than or level with the heart, but the consensus is that it should not be above it.

3. Make a note of the circumference of the limb at the bite site and at various points above the site as well. This will help you monitor swelling.

4. Evacuate your victim. Ideally he should be carried out to minimize movement. If the victim appears to be doing OK, he can walk. Stop and rest frequently, and if the swelling appears to be spreading or the patient's symptoms increase, change your plan and find a way to get your patient transported.

5. If you are waiting for rescue, make sure to keep your patient comfortable and hydrated (unless he begins vomiting).

Snakebite treatment is rife with old-fashioned remedies: You used to be told to cut and suck the venom out of the bite site or to use a suction cup extractor for the same purpose; applying an electric shock to the area was even in vogue for a while. Do not do any of these things. Do not apply ice, do not give your patient painkillers, and do not apply a tourniquet. All you really want to do is keep your patient calm and get help. If you're alone and have to hike out, don't run—you'll only increase the flow of blood throughout your system. Instead, walk calmly.

Dehydration. Have you ever hiked in hot weather and had a roaring headache and felt fatigued after only a few miles? More than likely you were dehydrated. Symptoms of dehydration include fatigue, headache, and decreased coordination and judgment. When you are hiking, your body's rate of fluid loss depends on the outside

temperature, humidity, altitude, and your activity level. On average, a hiker walking in warm weather will lose four liters of fluid a day. That fluid loss is easily replaced by normal consumption of liquids and food. However, if a hiker is walking briskly in hot, dry weather and hauling a heavy pack, he or she can lose one to three liters of water an hour. It's important to always carry plenty of water and to stop often and drink fluids regularly, even if you aren't thirsty.

Heat exhaustion is the result of a loss of large amounts of electrolytes and often occurs if a hiker is dehydrated and has been under heavy exertion. Common symptoms of heat exhaustion include cramping, exhaustion, fatigue, lightheadedness, and nausea. You can treat heat exhaustion by getting out of the sun and drinking an electrolyte solution made up of one teaspoon of salt and one tablespoon of sugar dissolved in a liter of water. Drink this solution slowly over a period of 1 hour. Drinking plenty of fluids (preferably an electrolyte solution/sports drink) can prevent heat exhaustion. Avoid hiking during the hottest parts of the day, and wear breathable clothing, a wide-brimmed hat, and sunglasses.

Hypothermia. Hypothermia is one of the biggest dangers in the backcountry, especially for day hikers in the summertime. That may sound strange, but imagine starting out on a hike in midsummer when it's sunny and 80°F out. You're clad in nylon shorts and a cotton T-shirt. About halfway through your hike, the sky begins to cloud up, and in the next hour a light drizzle begins to fall and the wind starts to pick up. Before you know it, you are soaking wet and shivering—the perfect recipe for hypothermia. More advanced signs include decreased coordination, slurred speech, and blurred vision. When a victim's temperature falls below 92°F, the blood pressure and pulse plummet, possibly leading to coma and death.

To avoid hypothermia, always bring a windproof, rainproof shell, a fleece jacket, long underwear made of a breathable, synthetic fiber, gloves, and a hat when you are hiking in the mountains. Learn to adjust your clothing layers based on the temperature. If you are climbing uphill at a moderate pace, you will stay warm, but when you stop for a break, you'll become cold quickly, unless you add more layers of clothing.

If a hiker is showing advanced signs of hypothermia, dress him or her in dry clothes and make sure he or she is wearing a hat and gloves. Place the person in a sleeping bag in a tent or shelter that will protect him or her from the wind and other elements. Give the person warm fluids to drink and keep him awake.

Frostbite. When the mercury dips below 32°F, your extremities begin to chill. If a persistent chill attacks a localized area, say, your hands or your toes, the circulatory system reacts by cutting off blood flow to the affected area—the idea being to protect and preserve the body's overall temperature. And so it's death by attrition for the affected area. Ice crystals start to form from the water in the cells of the neglected tissue. Deprived of heat, nourishment, and now water, the tissue literally starves. This is frostbite.

Prevention is your best defense against this situation. Most prone to frostbite are your face, hands, and feet, so protect these areas well. Wool is the traditional material

of choice because it provides ample air space for insulation and draws moisture away from the skin. Synthetic fabrics, however, have made great strides in the cold weather clothing market. Do your research. A pair of light silk liners under your regular gloves is a good trick for keeping warm. They afford some additional warmth, but more importantly they'll allow you to remove your mitts for tedious work without exposing the skin.

If your feet or hands start to feel cold or numb due to the elements, warm them as quickly as possible. Place cold hands under your armpits or bury them in your crotch. If your feet are cold, change your socks. If there's plenty of room in your boots, add another pair of socks. Do remember, though, that constricting your feet in tight boots can restrict blood flow and actually make your feet colder more quickly. Your socks need to have breathing room if they're going to be effective. Dead air provides insulation. If your face is cold, place your warm hands over your face, or simply wear a head stocking.

Should your skin go numb and start to appear white and waxy, chances are you've got or are developing frostbite. Don't try to thaw the area unless you can maintain the warmth. In other words don't stop to warm up your frostbitten feet only to head

Scarlet catchfly

back on the trail. You'll do more damage than good. Tests have shown that hikers who walked on thawed feet did more harm, and endured more pain, than hikers who left the affected areas alone. Do your best to get out of the cold entirely and seek medical attention—which usually consists of performing a rapid rewarming in water for 20 to 30 minutes.

The overall objective in preventing both hypothermia and frostbite is to keep the body's core warm. Protect key areas where heat escapes, like the top of the head, and maintain the proper nutrition level. Foods that are high in calories aid the body in producing heat. Never smoke or drink when you're in situations where the cold is threatening. By affecting blood flow, these activities ultimately cool the body's core temperature.

Hantavirus Pulmonary Syndrome (HPS). Deer mice spread the virus that causes HPS, and humans contract it from breathing it in, usually when they've disturbed an area with dust and mouse feces from nests or surfaces with mouse droppings or urine. Exposure to large numbers of rodents and their feces or urine presents the greatest risk. As hikers, we sometimes enter old buildings, and often deer mice live in these places. We may not be around long enough to be exposed, but do be aware of this disease. About half the people who develop HPS die. Symptoms are flulike and appear about two to three weeks after exposure. After initial symptoms a dry cough and shortness of breath follow. Breathing is difficult. If you even think you might have HPS, see a doctor immediately!

Natural Hazards

Besides tripping over a rock or tree root on the trail, there are some real hazards to be aware of while hiking. Even if where you're hiking doesn't have the plethora of poisonous snakes and plants, insects, and grizzly bears found in other parts of the United States, there are a few weather conditions and predators you may need to take into account.

Lightning. Thunderstorms build over the mountains almost every day during the summer. Lightning is generated by thunderheads and can strike without warning, even several miles away from the nearest overhead cloud. The best rule of thumb is to start leaving exposed peaks, ridges, and canyon rims by about noon. This time can vary a little depending on storm buildup. Keep an eye on cloud formation and don't underestimate how fast a storm can build. The bigger they get, the more likely a thunderstorm will happen. Lightning takes the path of least resistance, so if you're the highpoint, it might choose you. Ducking under a rock overhang is dangerous as you form the shortest path between the rock and ground. If you dash below tree line, avoid standing under the only or the tallest tree. If you are caught above tree line, stay away from anything metal you might be carrying, Move down off the ridge slightly to a low, treeless point and squat until the storm passes. If you have an insulating pad, squat on it. Avoid having both your hands and feet touching the ground at once and

never lie flat. If you hear a buzzing sound or feel your hair standing on end, move quickly as an electrical charge is building up.

Flash floods. Flash floods pose a threat to those hiking near many of the creeks described in this guide. Keep an eye on the weather and always climb to safety if danger threatens. Flash floods usually subside quickly, so be patient and don't cross a swollen stream.

Bears. Most of the United States (outside of the Pacific Northwest and parts of the Northern Rockies) does not have a grizzly bear population, although some rumors exist about sightings where there should be none. Black bears are plentiful, however. While sightings are rare, there are black bears in the Ozarks. Here are some tips in case you and a bear scare each other. Most of all, avoid surprising a bear. Talk or sing where visibility or hearing are limited, such as along a rushing creek or in thick brush. While hiking, watch for bear tracks (five toes), droppings (sizable with leaves, partly digested berries, seeds, and/or animal fur), or rocks and roots along the trail that show signs of being dug up (this could be a bear looking for bugs to eat). Keep a clean camp, hang food or use bear-proof storage containers, and don't sleep in the clothes you wore while cooking. Be especially careful to avoid getting between a mother and her cubs. In late summer and fall bears are busy eating to fatten up for winter, so be extra careful around berry bushes. If you do encounter a bear, move away slowly while facing the bear, talk softly, and avoid direct eye contact. Give the bear room to escape. Since bears are very curious, it might stand upright to get a better whiff of you, and it may even charge you to try to intimidate you. Try to stay calm. If a black bear attacks you, fight back with anything you have handy. Unleashed dogs have been known to come running back to their owners with a bear close behind. Keep your dog on a leash or within view at all times.

Mountain lions. It is extremely unlikely that you will see a mountain lion while hiking anywhere in the Midwest. With that being said, there have been a handful of confirmed mountain lion sightings in the Ozarks in recent years, including one confirmed sighting in St. Louis County in January 2011. Mountain lions appear to be getting more comfortable around humans as long as deer (their favorite prey) are in an area with adequate cover. Usually elusive and quiet, lions rarely attack people. If you meet a lion, give it a chance to escape. Stay calm and talk firmly to it. Back away slowly while facing the lion. If you run, you'll only encourage the cat to chase you. Make yourself look large by opening a jacket, if you have one, or waving your hiking poles. If the lion behaves aggressively, throw stones, sticks, or whatever you can while remaining tall. If a lion does attack, fight for your life with anything you can grab.

Other considerations. Hunting is a popular sport in the United States, especially during rut season in October and November. Hiking is still enjoyable in those months in many areas, so just take a few precautions. First, learn when the different hunting seasons start and end in the area in which you'll be hiking. During this time frame, be sure to wear at least a blaze orange hat, and possibly put an orange vest over your pack. Don't be surprised to see hunters in camo outfits carrying bows or rifles

around during their season. If you would feel more comfortable without hunters around, hike in national parks and monuments or state and local parks where hunting is not allowed.

Navigation

Whether you are going on a short hike in a familiar area or planning a weeklong backpack trip, you should always be equipped with the proper navigational equipment—at the very least a detailed map and a sturdy compass.

Maps. There are many different types of maps available to help you find your way on the trail. Easiest to find are Forest Service maps and BLM (Bureau of Land Management) maps. These maps tend to cover large areas, so be sure they are detailed enough for your particular trip. You can also obtain national park maps as well as high-quality maps from private companies and trail groups. These maps can be obtained either from outdoor stores or ranger stations.

U.S. Geological Survey topographic maps are particularly popular with hikers—especially serious backcountry hikers. These maps contain the standard map symbols such as roads, lakes, and rivers, as well as contour lines that show the details of the trail terrain like ridges, valleys, passes, and mountain peaks. The 7.5-minute series (1 inch on the map equals approximately ⅜ mile on the ground) provides the closest inspection available. USGS maps are available by mail (U.S. Geological Survey, Map Distribution Branch, PO Box 25286, Denver, CO 80225), or at usgs.gov.

If you want to check out the high-tech world of maps, you can purchase topographic maps on CD-ROM. These software-mapping programs let you select a route on your computer, print it out, then take it with you on the trail. Some software mapping programs let you insert symbols and labels, download waypoints from a GPS unit, and export the maps to other software programs.

The art of map reading is a skill that you can develop by first practicing in an area you are familiar with. To begin, orient the map so the map is lined up in the correct direction (e.g., north on the map is lined up with true north). Next, familiarize yourself with the map symbols and try to match them up with terrain features around you such as a high ridge, mountain peak, river, or lake. If you are practicing with a USGS map, notice the contour lines. On gentler terrain these contour lines are spaced farther apart, and on steeper terrain they are closer together. Pick a short loop trail, and stop frequently to check your position on the map. As you practice map reading, you'll learn how to anticipate a steep section on the trail or a good place to take a rest break, and so on.

Compasses. First off, the sun is not a substitute for a compass. So, what kind of compass should you have? Here are some characteristics you should look for: a rectangular base with detailed scales, a liquid-filled housing, protective housing, a sighting line on the mirror, luminous alignment and back-bearing arrows, a luminous north-seeking arrow, and a well-defined bezel ring.

You can learn compass basics by reading the detailed instructions included with your compass. If you want to fine-tune your compass skills, sign up for an orienteering class or purchase a book on compass reading. Once you've learned the basic skills of using a compass, remember to practice these skills before you head into the backcountry.

If you are a klutz at using a compass, you may be interested in checking out the technical wizardry of the GPS (Global Positioning System) device. The GPS was developed by the Pentagon and works off twenty-four NAVSTAR satellites, which were designed to guide missiles to their targets. A GPS device is a handheld unit that calculates your latitude and longitude with the easy press of a button. The Department of Defense used to scramble the satellite signals a bit to prevent civilians (and spies!) from getting extremely accurate readings, but that practice was discontinued in May 2000, and GPS units now provide nearly pinpoint accuracy (within 30 to 60 feet).

There are many different types of GPS units available and they range in price from $100 to $400. In general, all GPS units have a display screen and keypad where you input information. In addition to acting as a compass, the unit allows you to plot your route, easily retrace your path, track your traveling speed, find the mileage between waypoints, and calculate the total mileage of your route.

Mossy rockface on Trail Through Time

Before you purchase a GPS unit, keep in mind that these devices don't pick up signals indoors, in heavily wooded areas, on mountain peaks, or in deep valleys. Also, batteries can wear out or other technical problems can develop. A GPS unit should be used in conjunction with a map and compass, not in place of those items.

Pedometers. A pedometer is a small, clip-on unit with a digital display that calculates your hiking distance in miles or kilometers based on your walking stride. Some units also calculate the calories you burn and your total hiking time. Pedometers are available at most large outdoor stores and range in price from $20 to $40.

Trip Planning

Planning your hiking adventure begins with letting a friend or relative know your trip itinerary so they can call for help if you don't return at your scheduled time. Your next task is to make sure you are outfitted to experience the risks and rewards of the trail. This section highlights gear and clothing you may want to take with you to get the most out of your hike.

Day Hikes

- camera
- compass/GPS unit
- pedometer
- daypack
- first–aid kit
- food
- guidebook
- headlamp/flashlight with extra batteries and bulbs
- hat
- insect repellent
- knife/multipurpose tool
- map
- matches in waterproof container and fire starter
- fleece jacket
- rain gear
- space blanket
- sunglasses
- sunscreen
- swimsuit and/or fishing gear (if hiking to a lake)
- watch
- water
- water bottles/water hydration system

Overnight Trips

- backpack and waterproof rain cover
- backpacker's trowel
- bandanna
- biodegradable soap
- pot scrubber

- collapsible water container (two- to three-gallon capacity)
- clothing—extra wool socks, shirt, and shorts
- cook set/utensils
- ditty bags to store gear
- extra plastic resealable bags
- gaiters
- garbage bag
- bear canister or rope to hang food
- ground cloth
- journal/pen
- nylon rope to hang food
- long underwear
- permit (if required)
- rain jacket and pants
- sandals to wear around camp and to ford streams
- sleeping bag
- waterproof stuff sack
- sleeping pad
- small bath towel
- stove and fuel
- tent
- toiletry items
- water filter
- whistle

Equipment

With the outdoor market currently flooded with products, many of which are pure gimmickry, it seems impossible to both differentiate and choose. Do I really need a tropical-fish-lined collapsible shower? (No, you don't.) The only defense against the maddening quantity of items thrust in your face is to think practically—and to do so before you go shopping. The worst buys are impulsive buys. Since most name brands will differ only slightly in quality, it's best to know what you're looking for in terms of function. Buy only what you need. You will, don't forget, be carrying what you've bought on your back. Here are some things to keep in mind before you go shopping.

Clothes. Clothing is your armor against Mother Nature's little surprises. Hikers should be prepared for any possibility, especially when hiking in mountainous areas. Adequate rain protection and extra layers of clothing are a good idea. In summer a

wide-brimmed hat can help keep the sun at bay. In the winter months the first layer you'll want to wear is a "wicking" layer of long underwear that keeps perspiration away from your skin. Wear long underwear made from synthetic fibers that wick moisture away from the skin and draw it toward the next layer of clothing, where it then evaporates. Avoid wearing long underwear made of cotton as it is slow to dry and keeps moisture next to your skin.

The second layer you'll wear is the "insulating" layer. Aside from keeping you warm, this layer needs to "breathe" so you stay dry while hiking. A fabric that provides insulation and dries quickly is fleece. It's interesting to note that this one-of-a-kind fabric is made out of recycled plastic. Purchasing a zip-up jacket made of this material is highly recommended.

The last line of layering defense is the "shell" layer. You'll need some type of waterproof, windproof, breathable jacket that will fit over all of your other layers. It should have a large hood that fits over a hat. You'll also need a good pair of rain pants made from a similar waterproof, breathable fabric. Some Gore-Tex jackets cost as much as $500, but you should know that there are more affordable fabrics out there that work just as well.

Now that you've learned the basics of layering, you can't forget to protect your hands and face. In cold, windy, or rainy weather, you'll need a hat made of wool or fleece and insulated, waterproof gloves that will keep your hands warm and toasty. As mentioned earlier, buying an additional pair of light silk liners to wear under your regular gloves is a good idea.

Footwear. If you have any extra money to spend on your trip, put that money into boots or trail shoes. Poor shoes will bring a hike to a halt faster than anything else. To avoid this annoyance, buy shoes that provide support and are lightweight and flexible. A lightweight hiking boot is better than a heavy, leather mountaineering boot for most day hikes and backpacking. Trail running shoes that many people wear for hiking provide a little extra cushion. These running shoes are lighter, more flexible, and more breathable than hiking boots. If you know you'll be hiking in wet weather often, purchase boots or shoes with a Gore-Tex liner, which will help keep your feet dry.

When buying your boots, be sure to wear the same type of socks you'll be wearing on the trail. If the boots you're buying are for cold-weather hiking, try the boots on while wearing two pairs of socks. Speaking of socks, a good cold-weather sock combination is to wear a thinner sock made of wool or polypropylene covered by a heavier outer sock made of wool or a synthetic-and-wool mix. The inner sock protects the foot from the rubbing effects of the outer sock and prevents blisters. Many outdoor stores have some type of ramp to simulate hiking uphill and downhill. Be sure to take advantage of this test, as toe-jamming boot fronts can be very painful and debilitating on the downhill trek.

Once you've purchased your footwear, be sure to break them in before you hit the trail. New footwear is often stiff and needs to be stretched and molded to your foot.

Hiking poles. Hiking poles help with balance, and more importantly take pressure off your knees. The ones with shock absorbers are easier on your elbows and knees. Some poles even come with a camera attachment to be used as a monopod. And heaven forbid you meet a mountain lion, bear, or unfriendly dog, the poles can make you look a lot bigger.

Backpacks. No matter what type of hiking you do, you'll need a pack of some sort to carry the basic trail essentials. There are a variety of backpacks on the market, but let's first discuss what you intend to use it for. Day hikes or overnight trips?

If you plan on doing a day hike, a daypack should have some of the following characteristics: a padded hip belt that's at least 2 inches in diameter (avoid packs with only a small nylon piece of webbing for a hip belt); a chest strap (the chest strap helps stabilize the pack against your body); external pockets to carry water and other items that you want easy access to; an internal pocket to hold keys, a knife, a wallet, and other miscellaneous items; an external lashing system to hold a jacket; and, if you so desire, a hydration pocket for carrying a hydration system (which consists of a water bladder with an attachable drinking hose).

For short hikes, some hikers like to use a small, lightweight daypack to store just a camera, food, a compass, a map, and other trail essentials. Most of these lightweight daypacks have pockets for two water bottles and areas to store cell phones, snacks, and other items you will want to access easily.

If you intend to do an extended, overnight trip, there are multiple considerations. First off, you need to decide what kind of framed pack you want. There are two backpack types for backpacking: the internal frame and the external frame. An internal frame pack rests closer to your body, making it more stable and easier to balance when hiking over rough terrain. An external frame pack is just that, an aluminum frame attached to the exterior of the pack. Some hikers consider an external frame pack to be better for long backpack trips because it distributes the pack weight better and allows you to carry heavier loads. It's often easier to pack, and your gear is more accessible. It also offers better back ventilation in hot weather.

The most critical measurement for fitting a pack is torso length. The pack needs to rest evenly on your hips without sagging. A good pack will come in two or three sizes and have straps and hip belts that are adjustable according to your body size and characteristics.

When you purchase a backpack, go to an outdoor store with salespeople who are knowledgeable in how to properly fit a pack. Once the pack is fitted for you, load the pack with the amount of weight you plan on taking on the trail. The weight of the pack should be distributed evenly and you should be able to swing your arms and walk briskly without feeling out of balance. Another good technique for evaluating a pack is to walk up and down stairs and make quick turns to the right and to the left to be sure the pack doesn't feel out of balance. Other features that are nice to have on a backpack include a removable daypack or fanny pack, external pockets for extra water, and extra lash points to attach a jacket or other items.

Sleeping bags and pads. Sleeping bags are rated by temperature. You can purchase a bag made with synthetic insulation, or you can buy a goose down bag. Goose down bags are more expensive, but they have a higher insulating capacity by weight and will keep their loft longer. You'll want to purchase a bag with a temperature rating that fits the time of year and conditions you are most likely to camp in.

One caveat: The techno-standard for temperature ratings is far from perfect. Ratings vary from manufacturer to manufacturer, so to protect yourself you should purchase a bag rated 10° to 15°F below the temperature you expect to be camping in. Synthetic bags are more resistant to water than down bags, but many down bags are now made with a Gore-Tex shell that helps to repel water. Down bags are also more compressible than synthetic bags and take up less room in your pack, which is an important consideration if you are planning a multiday backpack trip. Features to look for in a sleeping bag include a mummy-style bag, a hood you can cinch down around your head in cold weather, and draft tubes along the zippers that help keep heat in and drafts out.

You'll also want a sleeping pad to provide padding and insulation from the cold ground. There are different types of sleeping pads available, from the more expensive self-inflating air mattresses to the less expensive closed-cell foam pads. Self-inflating air mattresses are usually heavier than closed-cell foam mattresses and are prone to punctures.

Tents. The tent is your home away from home while on the trail. It provides protection from wind, rain, snow, and insects. A three-season tent is a good choice for backpacking and can range in price from $100 to $500. These lightweight and versatile tents provide protection in all types of weather, except heavy snowstorms or high winds, and range in weight from four to eight pounds. Look for a tent that's easy to set up and will easily fit two people with gear. Dome-type tents usually offer more headroom and places to store gear. Other handy tent features include a vestibule where you can store wet boots and backpacks. Some nice-to-have items in a tent include interior pockets to store small items and lashing points to hang a clothesline. Most three-season tents also come with stakes so you can secure the tent in high winds. Before you purchase a tent, set it up and take it down a few times to be sure it is easy to handle. Also, sit inside the tent and make sure it has enough room for you and your gear.

Cell phones. Many hikers are carrying their cell phones into the backcountry these days in case of emergency. That's fine and good, but please know that cell phone coverage is often poor to nonexistent in valleys, canyons, and thick forest. More importantly, people have started to call for help because they're tired or lost. Let's go back to being prepared. You are responsible for yourself in the backcountry. Use your brain to avoid problems, and if you do encounter one, first use your brain to try to correct the situation. Only use your cell phone, if it works, in true emergencies. If it doesn't work down low in a valley, try hiking to a high point where you might get reception.

Hiking with children isn't a matter of how many miles you can cover or how much elevation gain you make in a day—it's about seeing and experiencing nature through their eyes.

Kids like to explore and have fun. They like to stop and point out bugs and plants, look under rocks, jump in puddles, and throw sticks. If you're taking a toddler or young child on a hike, start with a trail that you're familiar with. Trails that have interesting things for kids, like piles of leaves to play in or a small stream to wade through during the summer, will make the hike much more enjoyable for them and will keep them from getting bored.

You can keep your child's attention if you have a strategy before starting on the trail. Using games is not only an effective way to keep a child's attention, it's also a great way to teach him or her about nature. Quiz children on the names of plants and animals. Pick up a family-friendly outdoor hobby like Geocaching (geocaching .com) or Letterboxing (atlasquest.com), both of which combine the outdoors, clue solving, and treasure hunting. If your children are old enough, let them carry their own daypacks filled with snacks and water. So that you are sure to go at their pace and not yours, let them lead the way. Playing follow-the-leader works particularly well when you have a group of children. Have each child take a turn at being the leader.

With children, a lot of clothing is key. The only thing predictable about weather is that it will change. Especially in mountainous areas, weather can change dramatically in a very short time. Always bring extra clothing for children, regardless of the season. In the winter have your children wear wool socks and warm layers such as long underwear, a fleece jacket and hat, wool mittens, and good rain gear. It's not a bad idea to have these along in late fall and early spring as well. Good footwear is also important. A sturdy pair of high-top tennis shoes or lightweight hiking boots are the best bet for little ones. If you're hiking in the summer near a lake or stream, bring along a pair of old sneakers that your child can put on when he wants to go exploring in the water. Remember: When you're near any type of water, always watch your child at all times. Also, keep a close eye on a teething toddler who may decide a rock or leaf of poison oak is an interesting item to put in his or her mouth.

From spring through fall, you'll want your kids to wear wide-brimmed hats to keep their faces, heads, and ears protected from the hot sun. Also, make sure your children wear sunscreen at all times. Choose a brand without PABA—children have sensitive skin and may have an allergic reaction to sunscreen that contains PABA. If you are hiking with a child younger than six months, don't use sunscreen or insect repellent. Instead, be sure that his head, face, neck, and ears are protected from the sun with a wide-brimmed hat, and that all other skin exposed to the sun is protected with the appropriate clothing.

Remember that food is fun. Kids like snacks so it's important to bring a lot of munchies for the trail. Stopping often for snack breaks is a fun way to keep the trail

interesting. Raisins, apples, granola bars, crackers and cheese, cereal, and trail mix all make great snacks. Also, a few of their favorite candy treats can go a long way toward heading off a fit of fussing. If your child is old enough to carry her own backpack, let her fill it with some lightweight "comfort" items such as a doll, a small stuffed animal, or a little toy (you'll have to draw the line at bringing the ten-pound Tonka truck). If your kids don't like drinking water, you can bring some powdered drink mix or a juice box.

Avoid poorly designed child-carrying packs—you don't want to break your back carrying your child. Most child-carrying backpacks designed to hold a forty-pound child will contain a large carrying pocket to hold diapers and other items. Some have an optional rain/sun hood.

Hiking with Your Dog

Bringing your furry friend with you is always more fun than leaving him behind. Our canine pals make great trail buddies because they never complain and always make good company. Hiking with your dog can be a rewarding experience, especially if you plan ahead.

Getting your dog in shape. Before you plan outdoor adventures with your dog, make sure he's in shape for the trail. Getting your dog into shape takes the same discipline as getting yourself into shape, but luckily, your dog can get in shape with you. Take your dog with you on your daily runs or walks. If there is a park near your house, hit a tennis ball or play Frisbee with your dog.

Swimming is also an excellent way to get your dog into shape. If there is a lake or river near where you live and your dog likes the water, have him retrieve a tennis ball or stick. Gradually build your dog's stamina up over a two- to three-month period. A good rule of thumb is to assume that your dog will travel twice as far as you will on the trail. If you plan on doing a 5-mile hike, be sure your dog is in shape for a 10-mile hike.

Training your dog for the trail. Before you go on your first hiking adventure with your dog, be sure he has a firm grasp on the basics of canine etiquette and behavior. Make sure he can sit, lie down, stay, and come. One of the most important commands you can teach your canine pal is to "come" under any situation. It's easy for your friend's nose to lead him astray or possibly get him lost. Another helpful command is the "get behind" command. When you're on a hiking trail that's narrow, you can have your dog follow behind you when other trail users approach. Nothing is more bothersome than an enthusiastic dog that runs back and forth on the trail and disrupts the peace of the trail for others—or, worse, jumps up on other hikers and gets them muddy. When you see other trail users approaching you on the trail, give them the right of way by quietly stepping off the trail and making your dog lie down and stay until they pass.

Equipment. The most critical pieces of equipment you can invest in for your dog are proper identification and a sturdy leash. Flexi-leads work well for hiking because they give your dog more freedom to explore but still leave you in control.

Make sure your dog has identification that includes your name and address and a number for your veterinarian. Other forms of identification for your dog include a tattoo or a microchip. You should consult your veterinarian for more information on these last two options.

The next piece of equipment you'll want to consider is a pack for your dog. By no means should you hold all of your dog's essentials in your pack—let him carry his own gear! Dogs that are in good shape can carry 30 to 40 percent of their own weight.

Most packs are fitted by a dog's weight and girth measurement. Companies that make dog packs generally include guidelines to help you pick out the size that's right for your dog. Some characteristics to look for when purchasing a pack for your dog include a harness that contains two padded girth straps, a padded chest strap, leash attachments, removable saddle bags, internal water bladders, and external gear cords.

You can introduce your dog to the pack by first placing the empty pack on his back and letting him wear it around the yard. Keep an eye on him during this first introduction. He may decide to chew through the straps if you aren't watching him closely. Once he learns to treat the pack as an object of fun and not a foreign enemy, fill the pack evenly on both sides with a few ounces of dog food in resealable plastic bags. Have your dog wear his pack on your daily walks for a period of two to three weeks. Each week add a little more weight to the pack until your dog will accept carrying the maximum amount of weight he can carry.

You can also purchase collapsible water and dog food bowls for your dog. These bowls are lightweight and can easily be stashed into your pack or your dog's. If you are hiking on rocky terrain or in the snow, you can purchase footwear for your dog that will protect his feet from cuts and bruises.

Always carry plastic bags to remove feces from the trail. It is a courtesy to other trail users and helps protect local wildlife.

The following is a list of items to bring when you take your dog hiking: collapsible water bowls, a comb, a collar and a leash, dog food, plastic bags for feces, a dog pack, flea/tick powder, paw protection, water, and a first-aid kit that contains eye ointment, tweezers, scissors, stretchy foot wrap, gauze, antibacterial wash, sterile cotton tip applicators, antibiotic ointment, and cotton wrap.

First aid for your dog. Your dog is just as prone—if not more prone—to getting in trouble on the trail as you are, so be prepared. Here's a rundown of the more likely misfortunes that might befall your little friend.

Bees and wasps. If a bee or wasp stings your dog, remove the stinger with a pair of tweezers and place a mudpack or a cloth dipped in cold water over the affected area.

Porcupines. One good reason to keep your dog on a leash is to prevent him from getting a nose full of porcupine quills. You may be able to remove the quills with pliers, but a veterinarian is the best person to do this nasty job because most dogs need to be sedated.

Heatstroke. Avoid hiking with your dog in really hot weather. Dogs with heatstroke will pant excessively, lie down and refuse to get up, and become lethargic and disoriented. If your dog shows any of these signs on the trail, have him lie down in the shade. If you are near a stream, pour cool water over your dog's entire body to help bring his body temperature back to normal.

Heartworm. Dogs get heartworms from mosquitoes, which carry the disease in the prime mosquito months of July and August. Giving your dog a monthly pill prescribed by your veterinarian easily prevents this condition.

Plant pitfalls. If you have a long-haired dog, consider trimming the hair between his toes and giving him a summer haircut to help prevent plants from becoming tangled in your dog's fur. After every hike always look over your dog for burrs and other seeds—especially between his toes and in his ears.

Other plant hazards include burrs, thorns, thistles, and poison ivy. If you find any burrs or thistles on your dog, remove them as soon as possible before they become an unmanageable mat. Thorns can pierce a dog's foot and cause a great deal of pain. If you see that your dog is lame, stop and check his feet for thorns. Dogs are not immune to poison ivy and they can pick up the sticky, oily substance from the plant and transfer it to you.

Protect those paws. Be sure to keep your dog's nails trimmed so he avoids getting soft tissue or joint injuries. If your dog slows and refuses to go on, check to see that his paws aren't torn or worn. You can protect your dog's paws from trail hazards such as sharp gravel and thorns by purchasing dog boots. RuffWear makes an excellent pair that is both sturdy and stays on dogs' feet.

Sunburn. If your dog has light skin, he is an easy target for sunburn on his nose and other exposed skin areas. You can apply a nontoxic sunscreen to exposed skin areas that will help protect him from overexposure to the sun.

Ticks and fleas. Ticks can easily give your dog Lyme disease, as well as other diseases. Before you hit the trail, treat your dog with a flea and tick spray or powder. You can also ask your veterinarian about a once-a-month pour-on treatment that repels fleas and ticks.

Mosquitoes and deer flies. These little flying machines can do a job on your dog's snout and ears. Best bet is to spray your dog with repellent for horses to discourage both pests.

Giardia. Dogs can get giardia, which results in diarrhea. It is usually not debilitating, but it's definitely messy. A vaccine against giardia is available.

Mushrooms. Make sure your dog doesn't sample mushrooms along the trail. They could be poisonous to him, but he doesn't know that.

When you are finally ready to hit the trail with your dog, keep in mind that national parks and many wilderness areas do not allow dogs on trails. Your best bet is to hike in national forests, BLM lands, and state parks. Always call ahead to see what the restrictions are.

Hike Index

About the Authors

JD Tanner grew up playing and exploring in the hills of southern Illinois. He
has earned a degree in Outdoor Recreation from Southeast Missouri State
University and an advanced degree in
Outdoor Recreation from Southern
Illinois University in Carbondale. He
has traveled extensively throughout
the United States and is the Coordi-
nator for Outdoor Recreation at San
Juan College.

Emily Ressler-Tanner grew up split-
ting time between southeastern Missouri and southeastern Idaho. She
spent her early years fishing, hiking,
and camping with her family. In college she enjoyed trying out many new
outdoor activities and eventually graduated from Southern Illinois University in Carbondale with an advanced degree in Recreation Resource Administration.

Together they have climbed, hiked, paddled, and camped all over the United States.
They co-instructed college-level outdoor recreation courses for several years before
joining the staff at the Leave No Trace Center for Outdoor Ethics as Traveling Train-
ers. They currently reside in northwestern New Mexico in the Four Corners region.

FalconGuides they have written or revised include:
Best Easy Day Hikes Grand Staircase–Escalante (revised)
Best Easy Day Hikes Missouri Ozarks
Best Easy Day Hikes Springfield, Missouri
Best Easy Day Hikes St. Louis
Best Hikes Near St. Louis
Best Hikes Near Albuquerque
Hiking Grand Staircase–Escalante (revised)

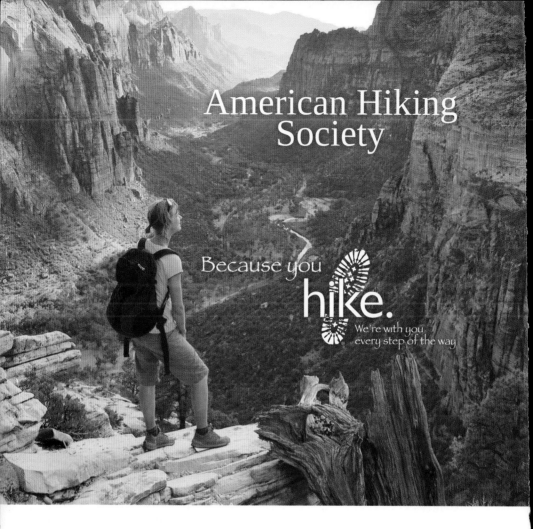

American Hiking Society

Because you **hike.**
We're with you every step of the way

As a national voice for hikers, **American Hiking Society** works every day:

- Building and maintaining hiking trails
- Educating and supporting hikers by providing information and resources
- Supporting hiking and trail organizations nationwide
- Speaking for hikers in the halls of Congress and with federal land managers

Whether you're a casual hiker or a seasoned backpacker, become a member of American Hiking Society and join the national hiking community! You'll enjoy great member benefits and help preserve the nation's hiking trails, so tomorrow's hike is even better than today's. We invite you to join us now!

American Hiking Society